A MANUAL FOR LIFE

FROM BABY STEPS TO A QUANTUM LEAP IN YOUR JOURNEY TO FREEDOM

TANIA DIMOV

EARTH ANGEL HOLISTIC HEALING

earthangelhh.com

authorHOUSE

AuthorHouse™
1663 Liberty Drive
Bloomington, IN 47403
www.authorhouse.com
Phone: 833-262-8899

Published by AuthorHouse 06/16/2021

ISBN: 978-1-6655-2857-3 (sc)
ISBN: 978-1-6655-2856-6 (e)

CONTENTS

INTRODUCTION

This little manual is dedicated to my grandchildren Cole and Liz, all my family members, and anyone who might feel a calling to unveil the mysteries of the soul and the purpose of their lives.

I don't know if I will have the opportunity to teach them all the lessons I learnt in this lifetime, so I am leaving this love legacy, little pieces of wisdom, which I hope they will be able to apply in their journey through life.

I also want them to know more about me, my real essence, which is reflected in every single page of this book.

This might also be a fun way to be always present, even when I'm gone, like an angel spreading her loving wings over her children.

This book is uncomplicated, written with simple words, in an "out of the box" style, so that people can grasp its metaphysical concepts and easily apply them in their practical lives.

My main goal with this work is to lift the veils of the mysteries of the universe one by one, to show how all cosmic principles function inside each one of us, and to teach how to open the right inner doors that will allow a much deeper integration with others, with all living things and the Great Spirit that created all there is—as above so below.

There is so much to cover that each chapter should be a separate book, but this little manual is just an invitation for you to open the first door to the exploration of the mysteries of our existence in a much deeper level than the way it is presented here.

If my words spark your curiosity enough to motivate you to learn more about your real self, my goal would be achieved.

We all spend too much time immersed in the struggles and distractions of our lives, that we end up forgetting who we really are and why we are here. As time passes by, we gradually lose the connection with our divine essence and are being led astray further and further from our dreams and our life purpose.

I hope these writings will also serve as an awakening tool and a call for what's important, for what really matters in life, so you can find motivation, excitement, and joy at every step of the way, embody the bliss of your existence, and create a life that's worth celebrating.

CHAPTER 1

THE ILLUSION

My first advice will be to be careful with all men-created systems designed to indoctrinate, program, control, and dominate the masses. Question everything.

The process of self-discovery is always a peeling of the layers of deception within and without us until the naked truth can be seen clearly.

Unfortunately, the negative aspect of human ego has corrupted all layers of society throughout the entire history of civilization. Greed and power-hungry systems were created to exploit, enslave, divide, and conquer.

Since the beginning of time, ancient sacred texts of all religions were corrupted and distorted to fit the mischievous hidden agendas of most religious institutions.

Power and control were the law. Kings, ruthless religious authorities, dark secret organizations, and greedy political systems were the source of all corruption, exploitation, and subjugation of the weak lower classes, that still in the present times are indoctrinated to accept, follow, obey, and serve. Authority was never questioned nor confronted, except in the case of a few minorities of brave rebels that were subdued and massacred by their oppressors.

Lemuria and Atlantis were the two main ancient civilizations that pre-dated all others. They left a precious legacy of wisdom before their destruction.

Some ancient documents, written with symbolic and allegoric languages to conceal and protect the truth, were decoded by the few spiritual masters and priests that survived the cataclysm, and their teachings were passed on to the disciples, in closed doors, secretly. These treasures survived generations after generations, always protected by their own concealed writings and esoteric occult symbology.

Whoever was initiated into these mysteries was able to decipher their meaning. Thanks to that, and to the few ones who were sent to the earth in a mission to serve and help humanity, these teachings can and will find all those who search the truth with a pure heart.

We all can see that until the present days not much has changed collectively. For the most part, the authorities of our leaders created a sick society with no equality, no love, no compassion, no empathy, no integration, no mercy.

We see empty unconscious individuals searching for the lost divine link, separated from nature by the distractions provided by modern and convenient AI hypnotic devices, exaggerated materialism, reductionist science, poor education, cruel economic inequality, indoctrinations of all kinds, mind control programs, and the seduction of all pleasures of the senses.

Sadly, we are completely programmed to pursue all things that alienate us from our divinity and our sovereign power. Now, the body becomes the Master and the Soul the slave. The positions are inverted, and the result is misery, emptiness, and chaos.

There's also another trap to mislead the few ones whose souls are begging for light. To quench their existential thirst and find "salvation," these individuals fall prey to the dogmas and precepts of "spiritual" organizations and religious cults that promise an eternal kingdom of Heaven. Such poor souls are promised to find love, peace, and eternal life and end up by finding their pockets empty.

The blind faith of the deceived masses has enriched billions of religious leaders for thousands and thousands of years. In the inquisition times, the Vatican was responsible for horrifying tortures, merciless massacres, and uncountable murders of innocent people. In the name of God, more people were killed than the sum of most wars together.

Fortunately, those who listen to the whispers of their souls, those who are able to see the falsehood of our matrix system, those who can look in the eyes of maya (the illusion) and find the concealed truth, those who can finally realize that there's something very wrong with the direction that our society is going, that, no matter how comfortable life might be, there's always an emptiness and a lack of meaning in our tridimensional materialistic perspective … these ones will knock and the doors for freedom will open.

We were created and designed to experiment this physical playground in order to have fun, to enjoy, and to experience the contrast of duality from which we should learn and evolve.

So, what went wrong? How did we fall into such a tremendous trap? How could we so easily fall prey to the negative aspects of our ego? How could we surrender our divinity, our sovereignty, and our free will to forces that don't have our best interests in mind? And worse, how could we practically beg that to happen?

CHAPTER 2

WHAT HAPPENS AT BIRTH?

Before we came into this world, we were sparkles of God's light that descended throughout all dimensions until it reached our physical plane.

In this descending process of materialization, Source Energy, the Great Spirit, spreads pieces of Itself throughout all dimensions of reality. These particles of divine light are called souls. Each soul contains all the divine properties of the Great Spirit, as a drop of ocean water contains the whole ocean in it. Each individuated body of light integrates into the dimension they are meant to exist.

Our whole body-mind complex is composed of many subtle light bodies; each one equipped to perceive the dimension they are supposed to interact. For example, the mental body exists in the mental plane but also perceives the astral and physical dimensions at the same time.

Each light body can perceive and interact with its own dimension and the dimensions that are "below" them but not the ones "above" them.

For the sake of practicality and a better understanding of the three lower dimensions, I will mention only our three lower light bodies as follows:

1. Mental light body – Mind – Mental realm – 5th dimension
2. Astral light body – Emotions – Astral realm – 4th dimension
3. Physical body – Physicality – Physical realm – 3rd dimension

When the soul incarnates in a physical body, she undergoes a process called "amnesia", since she loses the memory of all her previous lives. There

4

are many possible reasons for that to occur and this is a very polemic and controversial subject in the spiritual communities and religious teachings of all kinds.

Some say that the process of the densification of matter is so intense that the veils of forgetfulness fall upon the soul before her birth.

Others say that this is a field of experiences and challenges that the soul must undergo, to learn the lessons of life, and the amnesia is meant for her to focus her attention point into only one reality and only one life at a time to avoid distractions that might jeopardize her growth.

There are those who say that the younger souls' consciousness is not expanded enough to encompass the remembrance of all lives she ever lived, because it's a lot of data to be downloaded in a single individuated mind-body complex at once.

Others say that this is not a real experiment, since we live in a holographic world of illusions like a movie, in which we are just actors playing specific temporary roles to learn and evolve, and if the soul retains her past lives memories, she would not take it seriously and her experiment would be compromised.

There are even some conspiracy theorists who are heavily concentrated in the studies of the lower astral. They say that some dark shape-shifting alien races that are hijacking our planet took control of the afterlife astral region. Such parasitic entities are said to technologically erase the memories of the souls before incarnating into physicality.

This sounds to me like a horrible and hopeless scenario, and if there is any truth in it, I am convinced that it could apply only to the unsuspected souls who are afraid and completely lost in the lower astral plane. Their low consciousness and desperation for an external savior could attract all kinds of lower astral beings with nefarious intentions.

The amnesia phenomenon remains a mystery for most of us; however, I particularly believe that all versions carry some truth in them. However, there is one thing that I am absolutely convinced of: The more you evolve, the more you expand your consciousness, the more you will be able to REMEMBER who you are as a cosmic divine being.

As you grow, your consciousness expands more and more, liberating you from any hindrances that might block you from embodying your highest potential, your sovereign power of choice, and your complete freedom.

Nothing will be a limit for a liberated self-accomplished soul. Absolutely nothing.

You will know that the whole universe is inside you … you will know that you can be anywhere at any time at once, because it's all already there in you, because the time and the space does not exist, and because the only frontier that separates you from everything is your own limitation.

CHAPTER 3

THE EGO AND THE SOUL

At the moment of your first breath, a snapshot of the cosmic stellar conjunctions is taken, and such stars' alignment will directly influence the characteristics of your personality, or EGO.

Certain traits are then enhanced and magnified, while others are not so pronounced. This phenomenon is highly studied by astrology. The astrological chart of a person reflects his/her personality traits and behavioral tendencies in the different areas of their lives, and the constant movement of the stars and planets will influence such traits for their entire lives.

That's why the expression "rising above the stars" is indicative of the need to evolve to the point of becoming the masters of our egos in order to control our destiny.

At birth, the soul is given this very important tool called EGO, body consciousness, or artificial soul. Each person is given a different ego, as I described above, that corresponds to their unique astrological chart. This artificial soul is meant to be the soul's best helper in the execution of her mission in a particular incarnation. The ego traits are changed at each lifetime, as the position of the stars are different in each incarnation.

It's believed that the soul has the power to determine the characteristics of the ego she chose to have, before birth, in order to have a genuine chance for the achievement of the goals of her mission in a particular life. For example, if you were extremely arrogant and insensitive to other people's feelings in one lifetime, you might be compelled to choose next, an incarnation in which you come in a position of humiliation and abuse in order to develop humility and empathy towards our fellow brothers and sisters.

I have questions about how this process is depicted by most karma believer doctrines; however, I will leave my comments for a latter chapter about reincarnation and karma.

I even question the linearity of the concept of choice, since I believe that a person should really have total free will to choose when and how he or she is able to overcome the lessons of duality.

If you are being constantly reactive to all polarity extremes, your free will is obviously compromised by your myopic views of justice and your poor capacity of discernment. Therefore, despite the assumption that the free will of the souls must be respected, the idea of a soul being heavily influenced by astral "helpers" to create the blueprint for her next incarnation is not far-fetched.

And if you come into your new life with total amnesia, you won't even remember why you decided to come here in an incarnation of pain and suffering to begin with. So, the danger in this situation would be if the soul, due to ignorance, begins to accumulate new karmas on the top of the old ones, always repeating the same mistakes, and never having a fair chance to escape the reincarnation wheel. Does it ring a bell?

It all boils down to the same conclusion: If you want to be a sovereign being who is capable of wisely choose what's best for your life, either here or in the spiritual realms, you must EARN it.

A good beginning would be to learn how to be inquisitive and curious about the matters of the spirit, about the laws that are hidden behind the veils of ignorance and forgetfulness. Know thyself and you will know it all. Knowledge is power.

Why do you think there's so much chaos, misery, pain, violence, poverty, control, and manipulation in this world?

We spend life after life in this artificial construct that we call life, in this heavy body of flesh and bones, bounded captive by our ego desires and enslaved by the narrow perception of our five senses.

When we die, nothing changes because we did not do our homework while here. We remain the same person with the same limited beliefs, constantly being attracted to physicality again and again, because it's familiar and alluring to us, like a moth is attracted to the fire.

What happened to the ego that was divinely designed to help you manifest miracles and wonders in this physical realm?

For the most part, generations after generations, our parents, grandparents, great-grandparents, and our whole ancestral lineage were programmed and indoctrinated to obey and follow what's supposed to be right and what's supposed to be wrong, how they should think, feel, behave, and in what they should believe.

All teachings, education programs, media, propaganda, religious institutions, financial and political systems, entertainment industry, science, education, health systems, and all sort of social influences were directed towards the pursuit of selfish desires, power and control, the lower aspect of ego, the survival of the fittest, the attainment of superfluous material things, the shallow, the vain, the divide and conquer competitive mentality, the numbness of addictions, division, and fragmentation.

Our true nature was buried in the shadows of ignorance. The result is a society devoid of equality, compassion, empathy, unity, and love. Those who were raised by loving and mentally healthy parents and a caring family can count their blessings and their hearts should explode in gratitude.

Others chose to learn with their pain and traumas,

If they are smart enough to recognize that their ordeals are blessings in disguise. they can learn how to alchemize darkness into light and escape this dystopian nightmare. But we all must wake up for the call of the spirit or we will perpetuate this reality forever.

The negative aspect of our ego is responsible for the misery we attract into our lives. In our society, the EGO BECAME THE MASTER AND THE SOUL BECAME THE SLAVE. If we don't see this clearly, we won't stand a chance of long-lasting happiness.

We must discover all the programs that sabotaged and subverted the aspects of our ego, by being the conscious observer, a process called MINDFULNESS or ACUTE AWARENESS.

Then, little by little, begin to uproot them, bring them into light, and alchemize them with our intention.

The ego is a piece of the divine light with amnesia, fooled by the illusion of an extremely limited perception.

Because of our identification with our ego and our physical bodies, our precious gifts remain dormant in our DNA. Our obsolete traditional science recognized only two of the twelve strands of our DNA. The other ten strands were classified as "Junk DNA." Our gifts of clairvoyance, clairsentience, clairaudience, telepathy, tele-transportation, levitation, etc., all come from the forgotten ten strands that were ignored by our reductionist science. Our divine blueprint is magnificent, and we have unlimited powers, beyond imagination.

Here is a cute and helpful analogy to explain the journey of an incarnated soul in this planet.

This analogy describes a holographic universe in which our higher self creates a video game in the quantum field and sends pieces of itself that we call Avatars, in an illusory field of experiences.

The whole purpose of the game is to have experiences in a self-created scenario of illusions, in which the Avatar should overcome all challenges. The levels of difficulty of the challenges are created for the Avatar to learn and graduate to the next level until he wins or dies.

If he wins, the higher self begins the same game again but next time with different challenges, until again, the Avatar dies or passes to the next level. And this goes on and on, until the Avatar conquers all obstacles and the Higher Self wins.

In another version, the Avatar, called Peter, for instance, dies and another Avatar, let's say, Mary, enters the game to replace Peter.

So, Peter in the previous round is now Mary in the second, and this goes on and on.

In a third version, the higher self is playing another game, with different rules and obstacles, and using other type of Avatars, equipped with different set of skills to win the game.

The higher self can play as many games as he wants because he is the creator of the games to begin with.

At every game, he gets better and smarter; he learns through the experiences of the various Avatars and the various games. The more he plays, the better he gets.

The Avatars are totally identified with the game, since they are programmed just to follow its rules and conquer obstacles. They don't have any idea that there's a game player outside the game, with the remote control, determining all their moves, guiding them at every single step and helping them to overcome all challenges.

Of course, in this analogy, we are the Avatars, in our incarnations, trying to win the game of life, facing obstacles and challenges in a field of DUALITY and getting smarter as it goes.

Most human beings think death is the end and that there's no return. They are oblivious that we have a higher self, guiding us during the whole game, and that if we win, he wins.

The previous example of Peter and Mary, as one being reincarnation of the other in the same planet, is an analogy to depict our reincarnation cycles on earth as different people in different timelines.

In the case of Peter repeating the same game again, dying and returning to the same game, but smarter at every round, is to explain the theory of the soul coming back in time to relive the same life again and again to perfect, learn with the mistakes, doing it better at every round.

Haave you watched the movie "Groundhog Day"?

The other analogy in which the Higher Self creates another totally different game with other kind of Avatars, depicts other aspects of yourself experiencing incarnations in other planets or other dimensions of reality.

But who exactly is your higher self?

Your higher self, or oversoul, is the sum of all individual consciousness or aspects of you that exists in all dimensions of reality.

Imagine the knowledge and experiences of all the expressions of yourself throughout the universe… The collection of all the wisdom, feelings, and experiences of each one of them in one single consciousness. That's why the higher self is called "your perfected self."

The Avatar in this story is the ego and the higher self is the higher aspect of your soul.

ONCE UPON A TIME

"Once upon a time a very wise and powerful magician that lived in an etheric kingdom, hidden from our senses, felt the urge to expand his experiences and magical abilities to gain even more wisdom and divine clarity.

Because his kingdom was made of etheric elements, he was able to do wonders with his powerful mind. So, he decided to create a game in the lower realms that could satisfy his tremendous thirst for knowledge and his adventurous desire to unveil the hidden and mysterious secrets of existence in a different new world.

He chooses a lower and denser dimension to set up his game because a harsher environment would be more adequate to provide the challenges that would be needed to develop good warrior skills.

So, he took many identical pieces of himself and spread them along multiple different points in a linear line, called "time."

Each fragment of himself was an Avatar. When the Avatars entered this lower dimension, the energies were so dense that their memories were completely lost.

Some history tellers even say that the holographic game was highjacked by inter-dimensional dark wizards, that erased their memories and weakened their armors, so it would be even harder for the Avatars to win. But I leave up to the reader's imagination to guess what really happened.

So, with amnesia and separated by the illusory perception of "time," they were unaware of each other's existence and that all the Avatars were coexisting simultaneously.

Each Avatar believed that they were separate individuals, with no memory of their origins. All they knew was that the challenge of the game was to explore hidden lands and overcome the traps, dangers, and dark demons encountered in their journeys.

They had to remain alive as much as possible to collect some precious coins called "memory experiences".

The goal was to collect as many coins as possible since each coin was part of the lost Avatar's memories. So, at each battle, won or lost, they would gain a coin, regardless, if they never gave up and were always able to get back on the horse again. This way, the more coins they collect, the more chances they would have to recover their lost memories, piece by piece.

Every time they failed, they would get stuck in the game, and if they gave up, they would be kicked back at the earlier stages of the game. Eventually, the number of opportunities in the game would expire; the Avatar would die and come back in another game, with different challenges, and the whole adventure would repeat again and again.

Every time they returned, they would have zero coins, but they would be smarter, stronger, and more experienced than in the previous games, and the chances to win would be higher at every round.

Some few Avatars became so smart that they started to realize that most obstacles and dark monsters they encountered in the game were projections of their own fears, negative thoughts, and emotions. They began to discover their own creative powers for good and for bad. They learnt that the best way to defeat such demons was to stop creating and feeding them.

With the screams of their fears silenced, they were able to finally hear the voice of the king that was always trying to warn them and guide them in their journeys and battles.

They started to be guided from within.

They became infused with the magician's power and started to regain their sovereign mighty power back.

In the labyrinth of mirrors, they were able to recognize and find their projected images, and instead of fighting them, they turned them as allied forces, bending them to their advantage and doubling their strengths.

Thus, the duality battle of opposed forces began to disappear, the memory coins became more visible and easier to collect, and the Avatars' strength began to be directed towards what's real, instead of getting lost in illusionary imagery.

If just one Avatar was able to get to the finish line with his pocket full of coins, the time barrier would vanish and all the other Avatars would be integrated and merged back into the magician, the king, or the higher self, whatever you want to call him.

All Avatars would bring their coins and precious treasures of their own individual experiences into the "whole", and the king would reign supreme, richer, wiser, and much more powerful than before.

You are invited to create your own personal end to this story. Be creative, be inspired, be magic.

CHAPTER 4

THE ILLUSION OF TIME AND TIMELINES

Imagine that you have three identical objects, like a tree for instance, aligned horizontally in a grass field.

The one in the left we'll call the PAST, or tree number 1, the one in the middle we'll call the PRESENT, or tree number 2, and the one in the right we'll call the FUTURE, or tree number 3.

They are 6 feet apart.

It's believed that it takes some time to physically move between tree numbers 1, 2, and 3, respectively.

Now, imagine that there's a wall that separates you from all the trees. And a door with a keyhole from which you can pick what's on the other side.

The keyhole is your point of attention, the focus of your perception concentrated in one single point at a time.

You look through the keyhole and see only tree number 2, which is the present.

If you could move the keyhole to the left, you would be able to see tree number 1, the past. If you could move it to the right, you would see tree number 3, the future.

Now ... if you knock the whole wall down, you will immediately see tree numbers 1, 2, and 3 at the same time. Past, present, and future coexisting simultaneously.

You could concentrate on whatever tree you want while perceiving the other two and everything else around them.

So, what makes your perception frozen in the present is just your inability to perceive the whole picture, because your point of attention is cemented in the present (observing tree number 2 through the keyhole). That's why you believe the past is gone and the future is yet to happen.

Be aware that time does not move backwards nor forward. It's our point of attention, our focused perception that moves through linear time.

We move through time. Or we can train our point of attention to expand broad enough to capture the "all-encompassing."

I hope this analogy was helpful for you to understand a little better about the illusion of time.

Now, let's talk about TIMELINES. By understanding that all realities coexist simultaneously, it's easier to accept the idea of multiple sequences of alternate potential future possibilities permeating the quantum field. Our choices in the present are what will determine what timeline we'll navigate next, and these choices will depend on our VIBRATIONS. The present is our power moment.

By the law of attraction, we always experience the reality which is in more resonance with our vibrations: fear, despair, anger, lack, sadness, separation, or joy, love, compassion, unity, happiness, and abundance.

Because we are in a physical body, we perceive very little, 3 to 4 percent of the whole existence. We are in the third dimension of the creation kingdom. But we are multidimensional in our divine blueprint. So, awareness and expansion are the keys to open the door of infinite possibilities, miracles, and freedom.

The higher we vibrate, the faster the pulse of our energy, so it's accurate to say that time gets faster in the higher realms; therefore, we can also say that time is flexible. For instance, many years in 3D Earth could represent one hour in another more subtle realm or five minutes of our count in another.

By now, you might have already realized that our free will here in this planet is extremely restricted, right? Why?

Because our perception is also very limited. Most people are still stuck in the five senses prison of their egos. Their choices are easily manipulated, and they are very easy prey for deceit, control, and domination.

So, we could say that we practically have no free will at the moment, or at least very little.

Individual and collective timelines work in a very similar manner. By vibrational match, individuals are bound together in streams of energy, drawn to the most compatible timelines of their collective energies.

So, there are many possible future realities for many different groups of individuals.

The real free will begins when our perception starts to expand, enough to see the big picture. Then, we can become the masters of our destiny and choose wiser timelines that are more in alignment with the reality we wish to manifest for our future.

How much free will can you say you have now?

What steps can you take to conquer a real freedom?

What kind of world do you want to create? And what's the mindset to do it?

What do you have to let go or sacrifice to conquer your freedom?

How do you want to ride this ascension wave? Kicking and screaming because all you can see is fear, grief, and despair? Or gracefully and confidently because all you see in the big picture is perfection?

CHAPTER 5

YOUR AURA

Absolutely everything in the whole universe is VIBRATION.

The denser an object is, the slower its electromagnetic waves.

Pure light descends into matter by "densifying" itself. This process is known as "involution," while the opposite ascending process is called "evolution."

Electro means fire, magnetic means water. So, the soul also has a very intricate electromagnetic nature.

Every single cell of our body is concentrated energy. The movements of the electrons around the nucleus mirrors the same elliptical pattern as in our solar system, galaxy, and the whole universe, the microcosm and the macrocosm, respectively.

The triad of creation is composed of the polarities Positive – Masculine – (Yang), Negative – Feminine – (Yin), and Neutral that neutralizes both currents in the center. This triad is present in every single aspect of creation; therefore, we are a live representation of a mini cosmos.

Our right brain is of a negative polarity and translates the feminine aspects of receptiveness, high intuition, the capacity to download abstract concepts, and comprehend the intangible.

Our left brain is of a positive polarity and translates the masculine aspects of logic, outward impulses, linear/objective thinking, and comprehends physical concepts.

The positive and negative currents coming from the brain crosses in the middle, above the throat chakra, at the level of the nose, and runs through the whole body in such a way that the left side of our body is of a negative polarity and our right side is of a positive polarity. That's why it's said that our left hand receives, and our right hand gives.

Our body radiates a field of energy, commonly called as AURA. It expands and contracts, depending on the mood, state of mind, psychological and health conditions, or consciousness level of the individual.

Its average range is around 3 feet; however, there are enlightened individuals whose auras are expanded miles of distance. It's said that just one enlightened being can illuminate the whole world. There are masters, like some meditators and monks, that incarnate in this planet with the sole mission to serve as an antenna that downloads and radiates an incredible amount of light throughout the whole earth.

The expression "Light Quotient" is used to indicate how much cosmic light the body of an individual can hold. Don't forget, our bodies are cosmic batteries.

Clairvoyants and experts in reading auras can tell when a person is imbalanced or sick, through the colors, size, and conditions of the aura. Keep in mind that the colors of an aura can change from time to time, depending on the mental or emotional state of the person. Although each individual has a predominant auric color, this can change also with his/her spiritual development, so it's inaccurate to say that so and so has an aura of a particular color.

As you evolve spiritually and your energy level expands, your aura will reflect the colors of your higher chakras, predominantly.

A very common phenomenon occurs when the individual suffers a trauma or his/her energy field is "invaded" by external negative sources. In such cases, one can notice certain "holes" or ruptures in the aura's membrane, through which the person leaks energy or is being parasitized by lower astral vampires that syphon energy through the person's chakra system.

The aura membrane is a delicate electromagnetic field of energy, or "atomic screen," that envelops, protects, and keeps the integrity of the individuality of a person.

If it wasn't for this protection, the person's physical body would disintegrate, blend, and bleed out in the quantum field. This process is called physical death.

The main common ways the aura can be pierced are—

1. INTERCOURSE: In the act of intercourse, both auras are blended and mixed together and all the energies that one partner carries is passed on to the other. The auras open to receive both partner's energy.

I don't need to say more for you to understand what this means and how delicate and intricate is the act of lovemaking.

Promiscuous people tend to carry very negative lower astral beings that are attached to their energy field. The holes in the aura are an open portal and an invitation for all sort of demons and dark entities to "come to the party."

The orgasm carries the most potent divine light that you can imagine. It has the energy of creation. Through sex a new life is born. Sperm is the seed of life. No wonder there are so many dark predators ready to indulge in this precious and abundant feast.

My intention is not to spread fear, judge, or condemn sex. Far from that. Making love is the most powerful tool for transcendence. The light that this physical union generates has a tremendous creative power, and the wise ancients knew that. The science of sacred tantra was created from this knowledge. Unfortunately, most people that portray themselves as tantra teachers nowadays use it for their advantage or personal gain.

A good advice would be for you to be mindful when selecting a partner. Enjoy and respect the magnificence of this energy and use it in a loving and smart way.

You can even take advantage of the incredible creative power that lovemaking can bring to your life by using your intention to determine where this energy will go and for what purpose. For example, before lovemaking, you and your partner can decide and set the intention that this beautiful energy can be used to magnify the joy and celebration of the relationship, to direct the energy up towards the higher chakras for spiritual clarity, to dissolve an existing obstacle, or to send it to the whole planet for the betterment of humanity. The energy is yours … use it wisely.

It is of extreme importance for the man to see the woman as the embodiment of the "divine feminine," a goddess that's there to bring him uplifting pleasures by surrendering her best feminine attributes to him. It doesn't matter if it is temporary, for one night, a year, or for eternity. What matters is the reverence, the respect, and the appreciation that you show for her feminine qualities.

Learn how to use your masculine power like a warrior to protect and lead. Feel her flow, swim or float in her waters.

Every woman has a peculiar and unique energy. You can only discover her secrets if you forget about your image and focus on her beauty.

Be authentic, be proud of who you are, and don't look to impress. You are enough.

Make love with your entire being, not only with your lower chakras.

Use your senses and silence the intellect. Enjoy.

. At that moment you are both binding together your most precious gifts; make it worth it.

For the woman, my advice is to honor your energy, understand the royalty of its divine roots, feel confident in your power of seduction, and don't use it for self-validation or just to fulfill your emotional needs. See yourself as a Venus, an Isis, or an Aphrodite.

Honor his power and appreciate what he gives you.

Teach him how to dance to your music in a feminine way.

Love every aspect of yourself; surrender and allow him to dive into your waters. Let him sense and follow your flow; embrace his power and bring eternity into that moment.

2. DRUGS AND ALCOHOL: Heavy drugs and alcohol addictions cause a dangerous negative impact in the aura. In severe cases, the auric field expands artificially like an overinflated balloon. The auric membrane gets thinner, and the energies start to bleed out in the quantum field. This happens also because the individual's light quotient is not high enough to hold this "forced" expansion.

In the worst-case scenario, the membrane may rupture in many places and the person begins to present mental disorders. They can get crazy, lunatic, psychotic, or just can't differentiate what is real from what's not. When the protective "filters" are damaged, all the quantum data of many inter-dimensional realities is downloaded at the same time.

For the most part, what happens is that the addiction of these substances forces the electromagnetic field to expand artificially, and some areas of the aura are pierced, causing holes that are open portals to other dimensions. The veil that separates the physical reality and the astral plane disappears, and the person's "antenna" keeps broadcasting all the signals at once, like a radio with a broken "turn off" button, playing multiple stations at the same time.

There's a tremendous difference between having our aura expanded by natural spiritual practices as opposed to the artificial expansion by drugs or excessive alcohol.

In the first case, the person EARNS the privilege of the experience by his/her own merit, while in the other case, it's an undeserved borrowed power, stolen by the individual's ego.

One leads to liberation, the other to prison. There are no short cuts or cheating in spirituality.

Drugs can give you wings temporarily, but it always steal your Heaven.

3. BLACK MAGIC AND DARK ENTITIES CHANNELING: Possession can happen when you volunteer to surrender your body and mind to negative entities as a channel.

They might decide to be a permanent tenant and never move out, transforming your life in a living hell, tormenting you at every step of the way and inciting you to do all sort of things that you would normally disapprove, for their amusement or parasitic satisfaction.

In the case of black magic, agreements are made between the individual and a negative entity or group of entities, dark cults, demons, etc. ...

The negotiations aim to obtain their help to accomplish desired outcomes or material things.

You can imagine how this type of agreement will end. The incarnate individual always gets the burnt side of the stick in the bargain and the results are catastrophic. A very high price to pay for so little and a typical win-lose situation, in which you are the losing part, of course.

In some cases, the person involved in this kind of "give me power" game can never get out of the "agreement" because the dark astral wizards always have the upper hand and the advantage of much more knowledge in the manipulation of astral energies. It's like negotiating with the mafia of the underworld. They can enslave you for life.

What most people don't understand is that you are "signing an agreement" to another party every time you consent, agree, or surrender your free will to another external power, good or bad.

No one can hurt you if you don't give your consent. Acquiescence can put you in very dangerous situations.

. When an individual or a collective accepts a situation that is not in their best interest, they are saying: "Yes, you can do that to me or to us". Our society is purposely brainwashed to be subservient to authorities of any kind. Look around and think about that for a moment.

Be extremely careful with what you agree with, with what you accept, with what you unsuspectedly invite into your life...

Be vigilant and be sovereign.

CHAPTER 6

YOUR CHAKRA SYSTEM

What are chakras?

Chakras are energy portals or vortexes of energy located in your body.

Each chakra translates a level of consciousness that is corresponding to the many different areas of the individual's blueprint or psyche.

We have seven main chakras in our bodies and many transpersonal chakras "outside" our physical bodies. They go "upwards" from the top of our heads towards the cosmos and "downwards" from the sole of our feet down towards the earth.

Without entering in detail about the transpersonal chakras, it's enough to know that they correspond to your many light bodies and their specific related dimensions. But let's concentrate our attention into the seven body chakras for now:

1. ROOT CHAKRA: Color red.

This is our first chakra located in the very bottom of your spine.

Red represents the densest of all vibrations because it's related to the earth. It reflects your vital force, your vitality, your health, your body's primal energy, and your primal instincts.

The kundalini, which is the telluric energy of creation, is represented by a coiled serpent that sits at the bottom of the spine in this chakra. When the individual learns how to raise this powerful force up along all the other chakras, a tremendous awakening of powerful sleeping forces occurs.

The whole tantric science is based on this phenomenon and how to achieve illumination through this process.

The fight-or-flight response also comes from this chakra.

A weak root chakra might be a sign of poor health, low vitality, lack of energy, or apathy.

An overactive root chakra can indicate an inclination to primal instincts, fear, and reactiveness.

A balanced root chakra is a sign of good health, great vitality, and control over lower instincts.

2. SACRAL OR SEXUAL CHAKRA: Color orange, located in the lower pelvis.

It translates your sexuality and your creative power.

A weak sacral chakra might be a sign of low libido or sexual problems and that the creativity of the individual is blocked or suppressed.

An overactive sacral chakra can be indicative of promiscuity and uncontrolled impulses.

A balanced sacral chakra is a sign of healthy and balanced sexual energy and creative ability.

3. SOLAR PLEXUS CHAKRA: Color yellow. Located in your stomach area.

This is the house of our ego, our warrior chakra and our personal power as an individual.

A weak solar plexus chakra may be a sign of a passive personality, lack of self-worth, shyness, intimidation, or stomach problems.

An overactive solar plexus chakra might reflect some greed, arrogance, or excessive authoritarian behavior.

A balanced solar plexus chakra is indicative of courage, baldness, healthy ambition, determination, and good self-esteem.

4. HEART CHAKRA: Color green. Located at the level of the heart.

This chakra is all about your emotions and feelings.

The Higher Heart Chakra has a pinkish tone. It is located a little above the heart chakra and translates the higher emotions of unconditional love, compassion, and kindness.

A weak heart chakra might be a sign of heart issues or blockages in the person's emotional field.

An overactive heart chakra may indicate a lack of emotional control, propensity for drama and rage.

A balanced heart chakra is a sign of compassion, serenity, and balanced emotions.

The heart chakra is the "engine" of the soul, because it's the middle point between the lower and upper chakras or the point of transition between your lower aspects and your divine nature.

That's why most meditators are heart centered and use their higher heart as a bridge to achieve higher states of consciousness. The expression "sacred heart" says it all and even Jesus is usually depicted with a flaming heart in His chest that represents the flaming heart of pure compassion as well as the secret alchemy of transformation from the lower aspects to the highest through unconditional love.

5. THROAT CHAKRA: Color blue. Located on your throat.

The throat chakra is a portal for the manifestation through words. It's the communication chakra. Words create and manifest.

We must be extremely mindful of the words we speak because they are true portals to manifest realities, good or bad.

The voice carries sounds and sounds carry vibrations. Vibrations create realities.

The phenomenon called "Light Language" is the person's ability to download specific sounds, mantras, tones, chants or words that come directly from the sixth or seventh dimensions. These sounds carry a tremendous power of transmutation. It's the secret language of the universe, which cannot be understood with our linear mind. It touches the core of your being in a way that transforms and heals miraculously. It's a DNA upgrading for those who are open and receptive.

A blocked throat chakra may indicate that the person is bottling up the expression of his/her feelings. The words get stuck in the throat sometimes causing health issues.

An overactive throat chakra is found in compulsive talkers, lack of verbal control, or thyroid problems.

6. THIRD EYE CHAKRA: Color indigo. Located in the middle of your eyebrows.

This chakra represents your inner vision and the way you perceive reality.

A weak third eye chakra is a reflex of a narrow vision, limited perceptions and lack of clarity.

An overactive third eye chakra can be the case of the lunatics, day dreamers, and a propensity for alienation.

A balanced third eye chakra indicates a capacity to see beyond the material world.

When developed, clairvoyance is awakened, the individual begins to see the reality the way it is, not the way he/she is programmed to perceive. It's the capacity to see reality through the lenses of the spirit.

In the very middle of our brain, there's a gland called "Pineal Gland," which is directly related to the third eye chakra. When the Pineal is open and developed, all the "Siddhis" or spiritual gifts of the person are awakened. The act of "seeing" then is expanded throughout many dimensions and the naked truth can be perceived, without the veils of illusion.

7. CROWN CHAKRA: Color violet or bright white. Located on the top of our head.

This is a portal that connects you with the spirit. It's the bridge for the achievement of higher consciousness and illumination.

A blocked or weak crown chakra means that the spiritual connection of the person is severed.

An individual with the crown chakra open and developed can access higher states of consciousness and can connect with angels, guides, and higher beings.

He/she begins to download information from the higher realms and get guidance and protection from above.

Tapping into our multidimensionality allows us a much deeper connection with our higher self.

When illumination occurs, our consciousness merges with the consciousness of the universe and oneness is experienced.

Understanding the chakra system is vital for those who want to know themselves better, learn their connection with the universe, and use this knowledge towards their growth and fulfillment.

We can use this knowledge as a tool to align and balance our own energies, meditate on specific chakras to clear some aspects of ourselves that don't serve us anymore, heal illness and emotional issues, unblock limitations and open doors for our liberation.

We can learn how to elevate our primal instincts through some kundalini raising techniques, to transmute and alchemize the lower forces, making them work FOR US, instead of FROM US.

We will be able to recognize and identify the aspects of ourselves that are sabotaging our lives and use these powerful portals of consciousness to revert polarities and comply with our command.

This is called ALCHEMY. Those who master it possess the key for freedom and self-empowerment.

If we remain ignorant of our limitless potential and decide to ignore our capabilities, "someone else" will use them and take advantage of it, believe me. There are plenty of astral beings ready to use our portals for their advantage. If we could see with our eyes all that happens beyond physicality, I can guarantee that we would quickly shake our mental laziness off, take ownership of our gifts, and take over the driver's seat of our bodies, our minds, and our emotions. Why wait?

CHAPTER 7

ONENESS AND TRANSHUMANISM

Let's shed some clarity into a very misunderstood concept of what the mystics refer as unity consciousness or oneness.

We all carry the divine spark of light inside us, and in this sense, we can say we are all fruits of the same tree. However, certain religious dogmas or mind control systems of our society were purposely designed to lead us into a false light that illuminates a path towards a distorted sense of equality.

Transcendence is depicted as the merging of all individual consciousness into a SINGULARITY, or one cosmic mind, in which the distorted concept of wholeness means the annihilation of the self through the merging of the individuality into a sort of collective HIVE MIND, or I CLOUD.

This is not oneness. This is a dangerous path of destruction of our DIVINE ORGANIC NATURE and the fusion of all individual expressions under the control grip of the creators of TRANSHUMANISM. It's a path towards unconsciousness and automatization, a downgrade of our divinely created organic nature into a lower form of being, like a bio-cyborg.

We are all unique pieces of the same jewel, and we all are shining rays of multiple colors like a cosmic rainbow. We are the multiple faces of God. Our uniqueness is our beauty, our strength and our true power resides in our authenticity and our self-love.

Shedding our ego upon death doesn't mean the elimination of our individuality but the liberation and the expansion of it through the envelopment of all creation inside us.

We can contract and expand at will and can experience multiplicity without losing our individuality.

Oneness and unity come from the total acceptance of diversity and the total integration of the "Self" with all living things from an expanded heart space.

Love is the fabric of the universe and the great generator of life.

If we merge deeply into the dimension of love, we will be in the state of oneness.

Be vigilant and open your eyes to be able to discern falsity from truth. Love your uniqueness and make choices that allow it to be expressed freely.

The transhumanism agenda aims to end our human species as we know it and create a mechanical and obedient race of human cyborgs. Fiction? Unfortunately, not. This agenda is being forced upon us as I write these words.

It's already proven that the great majority of our thoughts, behaviors, emotions, and actions is a consequence of our matrix programs. We are already in a situation in which our behavioral patterns are so conditioned that it is very easy to predict how we will behave or react to different stimulus.

This human mental-emotional psychology has been used to subdue and control us for thousands of years, to such a point that we became enslaved by the prison of our own minds.

Most of our thoughts are not even ours anymore.

There's just a thin and pale stream of consciousness broadcasted by our real self that we can download and embody into our physicality. And this is not a new information. There are extensive studies that back up such affirmations.

Now, imagine if even this little door to our divinity is completely shut. What else will be left? What chances will we have to return to our divine organic nature through our own conscious efforts?

Artificial Intelligence is the queen of our era now. It can be used for wonderful purposes to heal, uplift, and serve humanity in many areas, but it can be also a double-edged sword that can be used for destruction. It all depends on the hands that hold it.

Unimaginable technological accomplishments are being achieved like the human brain connected and merged into a computer with the promise of incredible cures, a never dreamed hyper intelligence and amazing superpowers.

But at what price? Who is holding that power? Would you surrender your body, your health, your mind, your freedom, your soul, your free will, and your sovereignty to the commanders of the machine kingdom? For what reason? Fear? For a fake sense of security or the allurement of artificially created super abilities?

How does it sound to be 100 percent under the control of the matrix creators and have them decide what thoughts or emotions you should have and how you should behave?

f you allow them to judge and decide if you are a good obedient boy or girl, maybe you can have a little carrot tied up in front of your nose, so you can keep going peacefully and with no disturbances. How convenient and comfortable compliance is!

We can create miracles and wonders in our lives and choose expansive timelines in which we can explore unimaginable possibilities for our future. But for that to happen, we must see things with clarity, raise our vibrations, and take proactive actions to prevent what's being presented to us here in our 3D reality. And above all, understand that acquiescence, consent, and fear will cost our downfall to hell and the annihilation of our divine nature.

CHAPTER 8

OTHER DIMENSIONS AND YOUR LIGHT BODIES

We are multidimensional beings experiencing life in a tridimensional matrix. What that means is that we exist in a multitude of dimensions simultaneously. So, why do we perceive just this 3D physical reality? If our divine blueprint is designed to be so expanded and immortal, why are we confined into this heavy and constricted dimension?

It's because our point of attention, our focus of perception is anchored into physicality. Because perception is everything, and because since babies we were trained to be conditioned by physical laws. Our wings were cut, and we were not able to fly with our inner senses.

Our whole education system in all areas of our entire society is conditioned to perceive things in the same way, collectively.

There is a collective agreement for humanity to see, classify, decode, label, sense, taste, and feel this reality in a certain way. So, when you look at a table, for instance, everybody will agree with you that the object observed is a table.

But for a trained spiritual eye, this table is a portion of a quantum soup, that's an integral part of the whole spectrum of energy that permeates the whole universe.

This perceptual collective agreement is necessary for humans to function and operate in this realm, for practical reasons, because our little brains would not be able to retain so much data coming from all dimensions at once.

The problem is that the human attention began to dive deeper and deeper into matter and forgot about the soul's divine roots.

And as anything that doesn't receive enough attention tends to "disappear" from our perception, humans began to completely forget about the other dimensions that remained dormant inside their genetic codes.

As I mentioned before, the divine blueprint of our DNA has twelve strands, but our myopic reductionist science only recognizes two strands as functional part of the human genome. All the other ten strands are classified as "Junk DNA."

This is astounding because all our miraculous unlimited divine potential is within these rejected ten strands. So, our gold was tossed in the garbage, and we remain poor and miserable.

So, we live our lives on the tip of an iceberg, which represents 1 to 4 percent of all that is, totally oblivious about everything else that's under the water.

In this chapter, I will summarize the dimensions that we have the potential to perceive, as we evolve in our path towards enlightenment.

Some spiritual schools divide them into seven "layers," while others classify them into twelve. This is just a matter of cutting a cake into seven or twelve pieces … the cake remains the same.

Keep in mind that the cake is indivisible and there's no separation; the pieces analogy is just for the sake of our study.

Another good analogy would be an accordion that expands and contracts. When expanded, we can see the folders clearly, one by one, and when contracted, all of them disappear into one.

In a similar way, we have the whole universe inside us.

Every single cell of our body contains the whole universe, like a drop of the ocean contains the properties of the whole ocean in it.

Be aware that when I use the word DENSITY, I am referring to the entanglement of light within a certain vibrational rate. So, let's begin from the denser to the lighter densities:

1D – BEINGNESS/AWARENESS – Red Ray – Root Chakra
　　– All organic matter.
　　– Earth, Water, Fire, Air.
　　– Billions of years spent in timeless states of being.

2D – GROWTH/MOVEMENT – Orange Ray – Sacral Chakra
   – Chemical body.
   – All biological life – organic matter.
   – Microbial life, plants and animals.
   – Consciousness develops awareness through communication/ interaction.

3D – SELF-AWARENESS – Yellow Ray – Solar Plexus Chakra
   – Chemical Physical carbon-based body.
   – The birth of CHOICE.
   – Our current density level.
   – The shortest and most intense of all dimensions.
   – Introduction to polarity. The birth of duality.
   – Veil of forgetting.
   – The choice between polarities.

The 3D is the dimension we live in, the material world. It's the realm of the manifested thought or visible light spectrum and all that our five senses can perceive. Our perception tool is our material body.

4D – LOVE/UNDERSTANDING – Green Ray – Heart Chakra
   – Emotional astral body (chemical light body).
   – Average incarnation cycle, 90,000 years.
   – Full evolutionary cycle, 30 million years.
   – It's believed that the earth began to shift to 4D in 2012, and we will now begin to evolve into 4D bodies, from carbon-based to crystalline.

The fourth dimension is the astral blueprint for our reality.
Our 3D reality is formed by the "thought forms" that are condensed in the 4D realm.

5D – LIGHT/WISDOM – Blue Ray – Throat Chakra
   – Mental light body.
   – Balance of the heart towards service to others without being a martyr.
   – Learns the lessons of worthiness and unconditional love.
   – Develops powerful psychic abilities.

In 5D is where we'll find all probable realities available for us: all timelines that we can choose from. It's also called the MENTAL PLANE because it's the seed of all thought forms.

6D – UNITY/BALANCE – Indigo Ray – Third Eye Chakra
  – Light body.
  – Perfect balance between love and wisdom.
  – No trace of selfishness or service to self, only service to others.
  – Has the ability to turn backwards in time to all his previous incarnations to assist and help and then graduate to 7D.

7D – THE GATEWAY – Violet Ray – Crown Chakra
  – Light body.
  – If you divide our universe into seven dimensions, this will be the final density of our octave, or universe.
  – All personal memory/identity is absorbed into the whole.
  – These beings serve as guides/teachers to the higher self or sixth density.
  – One foot in time and one foot in eternity.

If we divide the dimensions into twelve, the 6D and 7D are dimensions of the sacred geometry, light, and sound.

The sacred geometry is the birth of the concept of form. The platonic solids are the base for all forms:

Geometric solids whose faces are all identical, regular polygons meeting at the same three-dimensional angles. These are the five-regular polyhedral; they consist of the tetrahedron or pyramid, cube, octahedron, dodecahedron, and icosahedron. The final divine artwork is the flower of life, which is the blueprint that is present in all creation. The Merkabah, which in Hebrew means "the Chariot of God," in sacred geometry, represents the divine human energy field. It's composed by two counter spinning tetrahedrons intersecting each other in the middle section.

The seed of the sacred geometry that gives birth to all creation is the vesica piscis, which is formed by the intersection of two identical spheres in a way that the center of each disk lies on the perimeter of the other.

That formation resembles the shape of a fish, that is where the name "vesica piscis" comes from.

Sound and color are powerful vibrations that can be used for healing or for the manifestation of anything you desire.

Every single note of the solfeggio carries a specific vibration. Those who master the science of sound healing are conductors of alchemic symphonies that resonate in the core of all living things, creating miracles at every note.

As explained above, the fifth dimension contains all probable realities for us as individuals.

The seventh dimension contains all probable realities for this universe.

In 8D is where you have access to the infinity of this universe as it relates to other universes.

The ninth dimension contains all probable realities for all universes.

Each dimension encompasses a bigger picture of the whole than the previous "lower" ones.

The tenth dimension is where the potential thought of God contracts down into a single point. It's the top level of the universal library.

The eleventh dimension is the ZERO POINT FIELD.

All the collective consciousness before their expression is merged with the Divine.

The twelfth dimension is pure bliss and oneness. Thoughts no longer exist.

I know that all these concepts might sound too metaphysical or intangible for a regular person, but the goal is to give a glimpse of the magnificent potential of our consciousness and how much we can achieve if we are aware of the potential we were given.

We were blessed with a divine godly creative power. We are invited to sit by God's side, in the Throne of Glory as the guardians of our universe and the keepers of our living library.

It says in the Bible that when God created Adam, the blueprint of humanity, most angels got jealous of his magnificence.

Adam's fall from grace is a symbolic representation of the collective soul of humanity descending into the abyss of matter.

The forbidden tree of good and evil represents the birth of duality, from which men should learn how to use free will to choose between polarities.

The serpent is the knowledge that allows us to distinguish good and evil.

It's time now to reclaim our real place in the universe, regain our lost treasures, and be the guardians of this beautiful planet.

In my view, the birth feels more like a death to me, since we descend from the etheric planes, abdicating our freedom, to dive into the unconsciousness of physicality, with amnesia.

Death would feel much more like a birth, leaving behind the heaviness of a dense body and flying to freedom and peace. A return to "home."

We should only be uncomfortable with the idea of death if we lived an empty life, full of regrets about what we haven't and should have done, if we had no courage to peel off the layers of falsehood, if we haven't embraced our authenticity, if we lived a life enslaved by our own limitations and fears, if we have failed to recognize our greatness, if we weren't able to see our image in our fellow brothers and sisters, and if we served the ego and ignored the cries of our soul.

I am sharing below two excerpts from some of my old writings. Surprisingly, both can fit perfectly well with the teachings of this chapter. I guess I never feared death because somehow my spirit remembers and misses the lightness and freedom of home.

"The Journey of a Soul"

Shot into a prison of flesh and bones, immersed in an ocean of forgetfulness, I descended into the abyss.

I experienced contraction, fragmentation, and division.

The sense of self is now blurred by the veil of ignorance and solitude.

I am a point of existence that was once shining and now lost its brilliance in the realm of darkness.

It's cold and harsh. Movement is heavy like swimming in the mud.

I look into the eyes of maya, the illusion, and I see the eternal search of the lost, through the outer movement of survival, conquest, domination, self-preservation, and struggle.

I felt the bitter taste of fear; I heard the cry of lustful desires, the yearn for completion, the grip of the attachments, and the thirst of the addictions.

Lost in the void, I was entrapped in the prison of an artificial construct called ego, in a foreign and unforgivable planet, moved by the essential substance of "lush."

Carnal beings coexisting in parasitism, cannibalism, and competition. The law of the strongest, divide and conquer, the "self" and the not "self" … domination, submission, and oppression. Numbness and amnesia.

I felt the anguish of pain and learnt the lessons of suffering.

I experienced friction, resistance, and denial.

Entrapped in the wheels of repetitions I returned here many times … until I could not take it anymore and the yearn for freedom exploded from the depths of my being.

The involution movement of the universe reached its bottom and the spiral of life reversed into its opposite, powered by my immense desire to come back "home".

Peeling off the layers of falsehood, one by one, I got lighter, and my brilliance returned.

Love and integration were my wings to freedom.

The point of light merged with the cosmic sun of immortality and now I AM.

The brightest light comes from the deepest darkness.

"No regrets"

If I had just one more day to live, I would laugh more and worry less …

I would look at all things in awe and gratitude. I would love more, forgive more, and forget all that's not.

I would say "I love you" more, I would touch more, hug more, and kiss more.

I would celebrate nature and be one with Mother Earth in all her expressions. I would dive deep into her womb and feel the beat of her heart in my chest.

I would revere simplicity and embrace emptiness.

I would fear nothing since nothing can be lost.

I would DO less and BE more.

I would trust more.

I would have nothing to regret and everything to celebrate.

I would be FREE, I would be LIGHT, I would be ME.

I would speak my truth and let the wind spread my words to the listening ears, so they will understand that LOVE is all there is and all that remains when everything is gone.

How liberating would it be if we all could live as if we had just one more day to live ...

CHAPTER 9

THOUGHT FORMS AND PARASITIC ENTITIES

The understanding of how thought forms are created, and how it affects us, is of crucial importance, so that we can have awareness of what we have been projecting into the collective morphic field for eons and are still doing it today.

Maybe this brief explanation will spark your curiosity and motivate you to research a little deeper on this fascinating subject.

I don't want to sound like a broken disk but let me repeat that the fabric of absolutely everything that exists and ever existed in the universe is VIBRATIONS.

In the last chapter, I explained about the many vibratory densities from pure spirit to matter. For now, let's concentrate into the basic three ones:

1. Mental plane = Our thoughts – Mental field
2. Emotional plane = Our emotions – Astral field
3. Physical plane = Physicality/Matter

The creative process is a descending force and materialization is a process of densification of the spirit, for lack of better words, into matter.

Therefore, we can say that OUR THOUGHTS AND OUR EMOTIONS CREATE OUR REALITY.

What we call THOUGHT FORMS are the concentration of energy in the mental field, projected into the astral, that are not completely materialized in the physicality.

If you begin to reinforce and feed them with repetitive thoughts repeatedly, you begin to bring into life a "being" that will have an independent existence, either positive or negative.

That's why it's said that we are powerful creative gods, or God's co-creators.

Such negative thought forms are commonly known as tulpas, demons, shadows, haunting ghosts, etc. …

The problem is that most people are oblivious of what they create, and the collective of humanity became a giant "Factory of Shadows," constantly polluting the astral with dark clouds of thought forms of anger, suffering, division and fragmentation of their own traumas, pains, and frustrations.

These floating astral forms are conglomerated in the lower astral, heavily influencing our minds and our behavioral patterns. So, we can also say that most thoughts we think are "not ours."

If we are unaware, and if our vibratory rate is low, we can invite these shadow thoughts into our energy field, because we became a VIBRATIONAL MATCH to them.

It's sad to realize that most of the time we walk around expressing opinions, emotions, and actions that are not even ours.

Subconscious and brainwashing mind control programs utilize this dark science to manipulate and use people to serve their selfish agendas.

For a society based on exploitation of the weak and the ignorant, the dumber the better, since they become easy to manipulate.

Some people are beginning to awake now and realize that we need changes immediately, but it's crucial to understand that we are not victims. We must stop this process from WITHIN, by realizing that our own creative power is being highjacked and used against us.

The only way to build a better society with equality, love, and abundance is to understand that the external reality that we want to change is a projection of our unconscious delegation of our own power to external sources and begin to take conscious ownership of what we want to create.

PARASITIC ENTITIES:

An ex-NASA scientist, dying of bone cancer, revealed what the NASA and US government have been hiding for a long time.

He said he didn't want to die in a way, having concealed this information from fellow humans. This is what he said:

"ARCHONS exist in our heads, in ideas, in our consciousness.

They exist in a cluster of negative thought forms known as PSYCH NEST.

Negative aliens exist within our thought patterns.

Some negative thought forms that we currently have may be a parasitic form of inter-dimensional life.

They reproduce themselves via LANGUAGE, things we say throughout the day.

They are fully telepathic. They can read our thoughts and implant thoughts into our brains.

Archons can travel through language. A process called TRANSMUTATION when they are shifted into SOUND FREQUENCIES.

Many major television stations transfer these beings by ended programs with specific frequencies.

Certain SOUND VIBRATIONS mixed with specific GEOMETRIC SHAPES create a GATE through which certain inter-dimensional beings can emerge in them."

For a person with average intelligence, I don't need to say more.

That explains well how vulnerable we might be when our repetitive thoughts are anchored in negative patterns.

CHAPTER 10

FREE WILL AND DESTINY

The most precious gift of all that was given to us by God is to be able to live in a free will universe. But do we use this gift?

Our choices are the brush that paint the reality we want to create on the blank canvas of our destiny. We are creative beings and evolution is only possible if this creative process is not suppressed, if our voices are not silenced, and if you are not enslaved by your own self-created limitations.

The worse form of enslavement is the one in which the prisoner is not aware of his chains.

If we are being sabotaged by our ego or external influences, if we are being allured by the false shine of shallow temptations, if the recognition of what's right and what's wrong, what's good and what's bad is never coming from our inner compass, and if the illusion that's presented to us is seen as real, how much free will do we have?

If we are lost, insecure, and do not know what we want, do we have free will?

An individual can only make smart use of his/her free will if the vision of the big picture is clear.

If you are on the top of a mountain looking down at all the cars driving on the road, you can see all the curves and obstacles and every single trajectory point from above. But the driver can see only what's immediately ahead. He doesn't have a clue what's behind the next curve.

So, the top of the mountain is your spiritual vision, the knowledge of your essence, and the awareness of the plans you made for your life before you incarnated in this plane. It represents the intuitive remembrance of your soul's aspirations.

If you are driving your car (body consciousness) on the road of life (the destiny prepared for your soul before birth), the only way to know what's ahead is to "be" at the top of the mountain, while driving your car down below.

How can you do that?

Using your intuition, your sovereign confidence, the connection with your higher self, and the capacity of spiritual discernment. If you are really in control of your destiny, you will know that there are infinite possibilities and unending timelines of probabilities for you to choose from.

So, if you evolve and grow enough in this lifetime, you will be able to choose whatever timeline you desire for your future. You don't need to stick or abide by any "contract" that you might have done with any kind of entity or "guides," before birth.

The idea of binding soul contracts, signed by the soul before birth, no matter how attractive or helpful it might seem, doesn't resonate well with me, and in my view, it doesn't sound empowering for the soul.

If you can see things from the top of the mountain, you might well decide to cancel or modify any pre-birth contract, declare your sovereign power, make your own choices, and be able to see clearly which road is the best for you to take. Your higher heart is your best GPS.

You are the master of your destiny. You are in the driver's seat and on the top of the mountain at the same time.

You have your inner compass that can predict the best road to take at any given moment of your life. Use it wisely.

CHAPTER 11

EMBRACING YOUR SHADOWS

What are shadows? And what's shadow work?

Shadows are all the aspects of ourselves that we are ashamed of, that we hate, that we disown, that we strive to forget and hide, that we ignore.

When we are ashamed of our undesirable traits, we are throwing in the garbage parts of ourselves that can be transformed into gold.

When we deny a part of us that is in the shadow, we are fragmenting a vital piece of our own being that's there for a reason.

If you ignore or suppress your shadows, you can never rise completely to the light. The forgotten parts of you will remain in misery and will be begging for integration and acceptance.

No piece of you should be left behind or buried in the dark. They will haunt you in your dreams and torture your senses.

By bringing a shadow aspect of yourself to the light of a higher understanding, love, acceptance, and compassion, you are embracing a part of you that's ready to be rescued, alchemized, and transmuted.

When you embrace humility and look at your shadows from a place of no judgment, you are fully accepting and integrating all parts of yourself into the whole. Nothing is left behind.

Forgive and accept yourself in your lowest and you will rise to your highest.

One of the most misunderstood concepts of many religions is the concept of forgiveness. It's imbued with so much guilt, separation, and judgement that it cripples the capacity of the individual to heal any wounds, shame, or pain of the unresolved traumas.

The self-flagellation, penitence, and the condemnation of the sinners were responsible for the misery of millions of devoted followers. The shadows were magnified to unimaginable proportions and the individual was doomed to deny and hide them forever, or they would never be forgiven.

Since childhood we were programmed to be a good boy or a good girl and taught how to behave in the right way or we wouldn't be accepted (nor loved). The "bad" parts of ourselves were judged and condemned, so we began to love only our "good parts." The "bad ones" were shameful. So, we went along in life, bringing with us just our good parts.

Whoever understands a little about polarities knows that everything on the face of the earth has its opposite counter polarity. Good and evil, white and black, love and hate, and so on.

But they also know that these are the extreme opposite sides of the same energy. Two sides of the same coin.

The positive side of rage is passion, the other side of hate is love, and the opposite side of contraction is expansion. But they are all extreme opposites of the same energy.

So, why not bring the opposite polarities into the Center?

This is the secret of the mystics that achieved the mastery of the self.

How can we love others if we don't love ourselves completely?

How can we forgive others if we are not able to forgive ourselves in our entirety?

When you embrace the part of you that you always perceived as "negative" into the central column of acceptance, love, and compassion, and when you recognize that it belongs to you, that it is a forgotten and misunderstood aspect of you that never had a fair chance to be brought to light, a miracle will happen.

Love and acceptance will integrate all parts of you, with no judgement, and they will be transformed into the most beautiful light of all. You will be able to reintegrate all parts of your divinity into the whole. And this is oneness. Search for all the sparkles of light that you lost in the darkness, rescue them and collect them inside your flaming heart ... and let the alchemy of love create miracles.

"The Caduceus of Hermes"

One of the esoteric symbols that mostly attracts me is the healing symbol of Hermes: two serpents swinging around the winged staff.

I see it as the most accurate representation of the cosmic dance of the two forces of duality: light and dark, positive and negative, attraction and repulsion ... the birth of movement.

In a constant formation of vertical infinity signs, it moves upwards, finding itself in the center, the zero point of neutrality and repeating its journey to the top again and again.

This delicate dance between polarities is a perfect inspiration and a divine message for us to find our balance and learn how to navigate the opposite forces that tend to tear us apart and pull us out of our center in the chaos of our physical existence.

How easy it is to get lost into our personal and collective dramas and how reactive our emotions are when we let ourselves be dragged by the triggers of the external circumstances.

This symbol teaches us how to gravitate always towards our center, how to dive into the shadows and then move into the light in a mathematical precision, in waves that mirror the opposite sides equally, gracefully, and harmoniously.

The problem is that we haven't mastered the art of this dance yet. We tend to stay too long on one side or on the other ... We sometimes reject one of the sides and often forget that there's a column in the middle that is there to support and integrate us with our divine verticality.

This is the perfect time to use this symbol as an inspiration to learn how to dance, to sense how long should we stay on the shadow side and how long should we stay on the light side, to achieve the perfect balance and allow the alchemic transformation to occur.

In the middle, we will find the zero point, the center of your vortex, the stillness, and the ascending force of your soul.

On the top, you will find the wings of freedom and the circle of eternity. Let's dance?

CHAPTER 12

THE POWER OF WORDS AND SOUNDS

In the previous chapters, I explained how manifestation in the physical reality a descending gradual process of concentration of energy that travels many dimensions until it crystallizes in matter, in our tridimensional world.

Sound travels in the exact same manner.

The words we speak are the final stage for the sound energy to manifest realities in our dimension. That means that we manifest our thoughts and emotions into our physical realm with the words we speak.

Jesus said that what matters is not what we put into our mouth but what comes out of it.

Negative words have a tremendous destructive power.

When someone says, "I hate you" or "You are worthless," that poor individual is cursed with a negative imprint that will have a horrible impact in his/her psyche.

Words are used all the time in subconscious mind programs, for good and for bad.

Imagine a child that is raised by abusive parents and constantly hears destructive words of disempowerment. What chances that poor child will have to be a healthy and confident individual in the future?

Any sound that comes out of our mouth that has a negative intent is black magic. You don't need to be a sorcerer to use black magic. We do it more often than we think.

Black magicians use words of enchantment, specific sound formulas, a combination of vowels, intonations, chants, spells, conjurations, phrases, and languages that are designed for different destructive purposes.

On the other hand, healers can use their voices to heal, transmute energies, and uplift the spirit.

An interesting example is light language, chants, mantras, invocations, harmonious melodies, and prayers.

Light language, also known in some religions as "Speaking in tongues through the Holy Spirit," is a completely foreign mysterious language that should be felt with the heart and the senses, instead of understood by the intellect.

The articulation of vowels and consonants intertwined with vocal sounds seem to affect the whole vibratory field of the individual, upgrading the DNA to a higher vibratory octave.

Sound frequencies are also used to activate the pineal gland, awakening its dormant potential, so that the spiritual vision is expanded. Binaural beats are frequently used for this purpose.

Each of our chakras have a specific sound frequency. The root chakra has slower, and deeper tones and the frequencies get higher as it goes up towards the crown chakra.

Instruments like tuning forks, singing bowls, and gongs can also be used to tune up the body energy. The repetition of mantras and the intonation of certain chants are often utilized to expand the mind or bring the individual into a state of spiritual trance.

The ancient Egyptians were masters in the use of sound frequencies, through instruments or voice. It's unthinkable what an experimented magician can do with this ancient art.

Sadly, in our materialistic and reductionist society, we tend to ignore, and even ridicule, this wisdom, and the power of sound frequencies is one of the many tools for enlightenment that is lost in the shadows of ignorance.

Be mindful of your words. Use them to raise your vibrations and the vibrations of others, sing more, and say words of kindness and appreciation to others. They are magical.

CHAPTER 13

THE SUBCONSCIOUS MIND

The brain has billions of neurons, and each individual neuron connects to thousands of others. Communication happens between them through small electrical currents that travel along the neurons and throughout enormous networks of brain circuits.

When all the neurons are activated, they produce electrical pulses in synchronized waves.

The four main types of brain wave frequencies are—

- BETA brain waves: Frequency 13 – 32 HZ. It's our alert state, or active thinking. It's our normal state when we are busy, thinking actively. Our cognitive mind responsible for Active conversation, making decisions, solving problems, focusing on a task and learning a new function .
- ALPHA brain waves – Frequency 8 – 13 HZ – States physically and mentally relaxed. Commonly found in relaxed states like in the practice of yoga, just before falling asleep, or when we are being creative or artistic.
- THETA brain waves – Frequency 4 – 8 HZ – State of creativity, insight, dreams, reduced alertness, deep meditation, lucid dreaming, and daydreaming.
- DELTA brain waves – Frequency 0.5 – 4 HZ – These are the slowest of all brain waves, when we are enjoying restorative sleep in a dreamless state, when healing and rejuvenation are stimulated.

Meditation is one of the most important tools to achieve acute awareness and elevated states of consciousness. It deepens your ability to focus and control your attention, and it can ignite expansive energy portals within you.

Breath work or pranayama is also a powerful tool to enhance self-awareness and mindfulness. The breath is the bridge that connects you with the spiritual world. Activities like pranayama or any other spiritual modality of breath work, yoga, some martial arts like Thai Chi, Qi Gong, and the ancient art of belly dancing, just to name a few, are highly recommended to increase your vital force and intensify your light quotient.

Now that we have an idea about the types of brain waves, let's talk about the subconscious.

When a child is born, the soul enters a brand-new body with a fresh perfect brain, like a blank canvas. The cognitive learning process then begins, so that the child learns how to identify and interact with the physical reality, according to the codes, rules, patterns, and agreements adopted by the human collective.

Until seven years old, the child's mind is like a sponge, ready to absorb and register all stimulus from the outside world.

The child can download programs, good or bad, just by observing the behaviors of the parents or other people. So, all learning processes are much more powerful in the early ages of an individual.

That's the reason why most traumas and negative programs that the person receives in childhood have a much more devastating effect, and in certain cases, the inflicted damages will persist for the rest of their lives, if not treated properly.

Our logical mind, located in the pre-frontal lobe of the brain, is responsible for our creative, cognitive, and logical thoughts. It's the thinker and the decision maker. The subconscious is the part of the mind that's not currently in focus awareness. It's just below the threshold of consciousness.

The subconscious mind is like a huge reservoir of information.

It's wired to store all memories of everything it learns, so that when the conscious mind gives a command, the subconscious is ready to pull out the stored corresponding file and execute the task impeccably, like riding a bike or driving a car, for example.

Such activities come out automatically without the need to think or analyze. The subconscious mind LEARNS BY REPETITION. That's why we see all TV commercials repeating at least three or more times the same message to make sure the information gets imprinted and recorded in the minds of the consumers.

The subconscious mind just OBEYS and EXECUTES. It's a brilliant and efficient helper and follows the programs that are downloaded into it. So, the conscious mind teaches and shows the subconscious how things are or must be done and then relaxes and waits for the task to be completed by its helper. A perfect marriage.

But because we are not mindful nor present, most of the time our cognitive mind is put on AUTOPILOT. We walk around pretty much like zombies in "la-la land," distracted and absent.

Somebody must take over the driver's seat, or the car will crash.

So, the subconscious takes over and does what it's trained to do.

The result is that the subconscious became responsible for a staggering 95 percent of the decisions in our lives, while the conscious mind is left with only 5 percent. And this is done automatically, like a record plays a song.

That means that 95 percent of our thoughts, feelings, decisions, actions, and reactions come from our PROGRAMS ... not from us. And that's all the subconscious mind is: stored files full of PROGRAMS.

Let me give you an example: If a woman dreams of becoming a ballerina and in her childhood her parents used to constantly undermine her talents, calling her fat, ungraceful, and clumsy, the subconscious mind jumps in and immediately sabotages her decision, playing the old, crippling program of her childhood.

The result is that she will be convinced that she is not talented enough nor graceful enough to be a ballerina. A lovely career aborted, and a beautiful dream shattered.

Needless to say, that when the subconscious stores too much negative information, these programs can ruin our lives, sabotage our dreams, and cripple our self-esteem.

A good tip to find out when or where your subconscious is mostly sabotaging you is to identify what area or areas of your life are failing to succeed and which are the repetitive undesirable patterns that you keep playing repeatedly. These will be the areas that you need to be mindful and willing to work on by erasing the negative programs and installing new and much more positive ones that will work for you, not against you.

Certain unwanted circumstances sometimes seem to be resurfacing often in our lives, and most likely, the villain of the story is the PROGRAM that was hacking the files of your subconscious for years and years, probably since childhood. Traumas in our childhood or at any point in our lives are also a bad "glitch" in the system and work in a similar manner, causing severe damage in the person's psyche.

Individuals that had loving parents and a healthy childhood usually have less difficulties to achieve their life goals, except if they were overindulged or spoiled in their upbringing. Excessive sense of entitlement and lack of appreciation are often the downfall of many.

The divine intelligence never fails and gives a fair chance to everyone equally, even if it doesn't seem that way on the surface.

There are many great souls that incarnate in horrible circumstances and suffer tremendous abuse in their childhood, but they learn how to alchemize all adversities in the fire of their spirit, like a phoenix that rises from the ashes.

There is an incredible amount of subconscious mind program techniques that are refined to unimaginable ways. Powerful hidden hands pull the strings of all governments, military, media, religions, entertainment industry, financial and health systems to control the masses.

We live in a trauma-based mind control society in which a minority of power-hungry oppressors manufactures fear, creates artificial scarcity for everyone, and conjures ways to keep us inside the prison of our own ignorance.

These hidden hands are the puppeteers that have been manipulating and deceiving the collective, generations after generations. Our subconscious panic buttons are pressed every time they want to activate the fight-or-flight response and trigger our limbic system to react in very predictive ways that will fit the controllers' satanic agendas. How clever, and how well they know about human nature.

WE ARE OUR PERCEPTION. Literally. What we think about ourselves, and the world will determine our thoughts, emotions, and actions that carry the power to change the world for good or for bad. The problem begins when we look at reality through the lenses of our limiting programs and our distorted belief systems. This is what will turn us into a very easy prey for deceit and manipulation.

The science of subconscious mind programming can be the most effective tool for empowerment and freedom, as well as be utilized for destruction and annihilation.

There are many healing practices that utilize helpful tools to replace old limiting programs by positive and empowering ones. I resonate with all intuitive segments of the spiritual branch of psychology that are not exclusively restricted to ego analysis, because they dive deeper into the soul mysteries.

Hypnosis, Neuro-linguistic, Psy-k, Kinesiology, Past life regression, Ancestral line clearing, Intuitive life coaching, Akashic Records reading and Remote viewing, are some of the many types of therapies available.

Mindful meditation, being in the present, focusing on gratitude, the use of creative visualization, repetition of positive words of affirmations, energy work, binaural beats, breath work are also some of the many tools used to reprogram the subconscious.

The THETA brain waves are the key to access the subconscious, because when the individual is vibrating in Theta waves, the desired program can bypass the conscious mind straight into the subconscious with practically no resistance.

That's the reason why all hypnotists induce the person into THETA first, and then begin the process of deprogramming and reprogramming the subconscious.

In THETA, the mind is ready to receive new programs intended to build new neuropathways in the brain, so that new venues for new behaviors and habits can be created.

My intention is not to overwhelm you with arid information but to show you how heavily programmed we are, and that most of our negative habits, repetitive patterns of behaviors, and false perceptions are a result of negative programs imprinted in our brains since early age.

I want you to know that it's possible to revert this damage, remove all hindrances to your success, and decide what programs you want to download in this miraculous bio-device to build the life of your dreams. As I said before, Knowledge is power.

CHAPTER 14

AKASHIC RECORDS

This is a short chapter to explain what the ancients used to call "The Book of Life," or Akashic Records.

Akashic Records are a symbolic representation of every thought that ever existed and will ever exist in the universe, collectively and individually.

All human actions, thoughts, words, emotions, and intents ever to have occurred in the past, present, or future are recorded in this etheric plane. One can say it's the mind of God expressing itself in holographic symbology.

Accessing your Akashic Records means you can increase your vibratory rate to be a match to higher dimensions of reality. It can help you to bring awareness of past events, revealing underlying unconscious traumas lived in the past of your current life, or past lives, that are blocking you from achieving your highest potential.

The Akasha is a library of earth's history, the collective of humanity and each individual separately. It's all there, like a giant etheric computer.

I already mentioned before that the perception of time is a creation of the human mind to understand and explain the succession of events that take place in our tridimensional plane, in a linear fashion.

So, when we access the Book of Life, past, present, and future are there, simultaneously. This means that you can "read" any record, any information of any event at any point you desire, either your present, your past, or your future timelines probabilities.

We can assess the records by meditation, creative visualization, hypnosis, vivid dreams, astral travel, and remote viewing. It's simpler than it appears.

Sit calmly, relax, put your mind into Theta, if possible, or at least Alpha. Set the intention on your particular "issue" or the answers you want to get from the records and go.

Be aware that this is a sacred "space" and that there are light beings who are guardians of the Akashic Records. They are there to give you permission to access the records and help you to get the answers you need to assist you in your evolutionary path.

Certain Akashic readers utilize formulas, invocations, or prayers to ask permission to enter this etheric temple. I just use deep meditation and creative visualization to induce my mind into Theta.

Then I visualize a holographic movie in my mental screen and allow my consciousness to enter this sacred space.

The most important thing is the reverence, humility, a pure heart, and a deep gratitude for the gift you are about to receive.

Before you feel compelled to explore this divine tool, I strongly recommend that you study, research, and learn much more about the Akashic Records and how to access them. But be aware that no protocols are needed to enter a world that's already inside you.

Keep in mind that the keepers of the Akashic Records are also a magnified expression of yourself in higher planes. It's all inside you, projected in the outside through symbology.

Angels, guides, and all beings of light express themselves in many ways ... through colors, symbols, sensations, geometric figures, sound vibrations, animals, angels with wings, humanoid luminous shapes, the figure of a master, or just pure light.

They frequently use your beliefs and symbolic representations that you are familiar and feel comfortable with.

The higher the dimension they come from, the less material their expressions are. In Hinduism, the word "arupa" means a world with no form.

CHAPTER 15

THE LAW OF ATTRACTION

Our universe is absolute abundance. Nothing lacks in the quantum field. All we need is already in us and around us.

We are part of it, and we are it.

If this is true, why most people are not able to get what they want?

Why there are so many in poverty, pain, and misery?

Why so much lack? Why most of the time it seems that the universe is denying your requests or ignoring your prayers?

There is an overwhelming number of books, teachings, and spiritual material saying that the universe has everything in store for you and all you need to do is ASK. They teach you how to set up your intention, how to visualize the object of your dreams, how to send the message to the universe, and they guarantee that if you do it right, you will be given anything you want.

This is right; however, there's just one vital thing they forget:

- The universe is VIBRATIONS.
- In order to get what you want, you must become a VIBRATIONAL MATCH to the object of your desires.

In other words, YOU HAVE TO BECOME WHAT YOU WANT TO ATTRACT. As simple as that. No cheating. This is the magic wand that will make your dreams come true, and if you leave this out of the equation, it's like trying to cook a soup without water.

Have you ever seen a very out-of-shape person winning a marathon?

Are you able to become prosperous if you sit in front of the TV eating popcorn the whole day?

Can you attract a handsome, successful, and generous boyfriend, or girlfriend, if you are the total opposite?

Can you be loved and accepted by others if you don't love yourself and keep criticizing everyone?

Again, everything we dream of is already in us, seeded in our potential, but if we don't water, the seed will die and will never become a flower.

We are blessed and rich beyond our wildest dreams.

If we have a box full of precious jewels but never use them, most likely you will lose or someone else will take them.

That's how the universe operates. It recognizes your vibrations and MATCHES them with identical vibrations. IT MIRRORS WHO YOU ARE. This is the law of attraction.

You might ask: What about these people that are so unfortunate at birth, or all the cases of birth defects, or many other misfortunes that accompany the soul when they are born? How can they possibly achieve their dreams if they are doomed by birth or cursed by fate to be miserable?

Don't forget that for most souls, this is not their first trip into this earth.

The soul brings all her experiences, all her limiting beliefs, all her bad habits and traits from previous incarnations into the new one.

We carry with us everything we are either in this body or in the spiritual world. It's up to us to cleanse old karmas, overcome old limitations, and learn how to step out of all the anti-evolutionary activities that were part of our consciousness before and still haunt us life after life.

Knowing ourselves resembles much more like a process of peeling off, "unlearning" old programs, and letting go of the attachments that we are used to cling on to, sometimes carrying our baggage for many lives.

I know in my core that when all those unpleasant lessons are learnt, the "unfair" limitations will be gone like magic.

We are our justice. We carry inside us the judge and the defendant.

WE ARE NOT VICTIMS.

Undress everything you don't need anymore, detach from all falsity, let go of the resentments, all traumatic experiences, your self-pity, and victimhood. Forgive, forget, and let go … detach yourself from the results.

Then, ask. And you will receive all the treasures that were once denied.

Is a father unfair when he takes a knife out of the baby's hands? Or when he prevents him to stick his finger into an outlet?

When the student is ready, the Master appears. Not before.

CHAPTER 16

KARMA X CAUSE AND EFFECT

The concept of karma is one of the most controversial in spirituality, till present days.

Most religions depict karma as a PUNISHMENT/REWARD system in which the colors of duality are heavily imprinted in the teachings.

God is depicted as a vengeful masculine being that rewards those who adore, fear, and serve Him in blind faith, comply, and obey His commands, follow what's thought to be right, and avoid at all costs what's thought to be wrong.

Whoever steps out of the line, the wrath of this unmerciful God will strike them like a thunder.

In Catholicism, for instance, you are born in original sin and will remain in sin if you are not baptized, and if you don't repent, you will burn in Hell temporarily, until you learn the hard lessons, or for eternity, depending on how bad you were when alive.

Some eastern religions paint karma as a tool that gives you the opportunity to come back to Earth endless times, and in order to be able to "fix" your mistakes and learn the lessons you need to evolve, you must endure the same pain and suffering that you inflicted to others during your previous life.

"An eye for an eye, a tooth for a tooth." You are supposed to reincarnate as many times as necessary, life after life, enduring endless punishments and paybacks, until you learn, purify your sins, and only then you will be able to graduate and escape the Samsara Wheel.

Supposedly, you are meant to plan the scenario of your next life before you come to earth, in which you will meet all the people you hurt or were hurt by and haven't forgiven. And the soap opera narrative goes on and on, in creative ways with actors and actresses playing different roles, until everybody is even, and all karma is burnt.

After countless incarnations of amnesia and punishments, if you finally succeed in paying all your debts and get karma free, you will receive a beautiful ticket to Heaven and follow your evolutionary path towards illumination in the higher dimensional spheres of consciousness.

How does that sound to you?

This sounds to me like a kindergarten horror movie, where the soul comes into this world with amnesia and has absolutely no recollection of her previous life mistakes, then is meant to follow a path of hard learning through pain and punishment, without having a clue about the reasons for her misfortune.

Most likely, the traumas caused by all suffering and punishments, plus amnesia, are more than enough to prevent the soul from learning and evolving. On the contrary, it would be the perfect scenario for the poor soul to make even more mistakes, accumulating piles and piles of new karmas on the top of the old ones, unconsciously repeating a never-ending loop of reincarnations for eternity. And sadly, most do.

The desire of "making things right next time" is the main motivation and the driving force to induce the soul to reincarnate. This, to me, is a cosmic trap, and the catastrophic result of a terrible brainwashing indoctrination based on GUILT and SHAME. Self-flagellating chastises imposed upon a soul that should deserve a fair chance for evolution and growth instead.

God to me has all polarities, not only male.

The description of a dominating all-powerful external masculine God comes from the old Kali Yuga era, a culture that cultivated the divide-conquer-dominate mentality. God is male, female, and neutral. So, a better denomination would be "Source Energy," because this word implies no gender connotation and means "the beginning of all that is."

It's evident that everything you do, every single action, will have a proportional reaction in the quantum field. This is science.

But because energy has no "morality", just polarity, every action that carries a negative polarity will result in an equally negative returning movement back from the cosmos, so to speak. And the same happens with the positively polarized actions. They will return to you, somehow, at any given time.

Because we live in a space-time-continuum linear reality, created by our own thoughts and beliefs, the aspect of this tridimensional plane is very dense. So we can say that in this earthly dimension, the "bouncing back" movement of our actions take some time to occur; in better words, we might take an action, positive or negative, and we'll only perceive its results after some time. It could be instantaneous, it could take hours, days, years, a lifetime, or it could even occur in a future incarnation. This is all that karma is.

The true meaning of karma to me is the universal law of cause and effect, the movement of polarized actions of an individual that reverberates in the cosmos, causing a counteraction that might occur at any given moment in our linear time.

So, it's accurate to conclude that you are responsible for the consequences of your actions and choices. Period.

All that old, limiting concepts that link karma to guilt and punishment must be mopped away from our minds. It just creates more chaos and self-flagellation that will ruin your real chances for growth and evolution.

Yes, we must be able to feel the pain we caused to others deep inside our hearts, in such a way that the act of genuine REPENTANCE is the element of transformation that carries the awareness that we are a different person now than the person who committed the "sin." Not because of guilt or a shameful self-flagellation but because we understand that if we love ourselves, we will be able to love others, if we forgive ourselves, we will be able to forgive others.

We are our own hell and our own heaven.

Our own consciousness is our judge. Not a vengeful God.

All relationships, with no exceptions, work like a mirror, somehow. There's always an aspect of you reflected in the other.

Human beings are made of the same "cosmic soup," just the proportion of the ingredients is a little different from person to person.

So, when you get triggered by someone else's characteristics, know that inside yourself there's a recognition of a familiar undesirable hidden aspect of you, in this or another lifetime. It's a call for awareness and a deeper understanding of your own unresolved shadows that are waving at you in order to be cleared.

Karma is intrinsically related to ego. The more you act and react based on your ego's narrow perceptions, the more you perpetuate karma.

So, in a way, karma is ingrained in the ego's structure as an automatic self-generating mechanism of cosmic "justice."

Visualize all the fragments of your higher self-projected simultaneously along the linear line of time. All the incarnated "selves" are interconnected in the NOW MOMENT and affecting each other by the vibrations of their thoughts, emotions, and actions.

It's easy to conclude that whatever you do in your present, also impacts your other "selves," positively or negatively.

Karma and ego exist because duality exists. Duality is the eternal pendular swing between right and wrong, good and bad, etc. that's present in our physical world of contrasts.

The constant pendular pull of polarities drags us into the instability of fragmented states of perception.

If you evolve to the point of subduing your ego under the domain of your higher self, duality disappears, and you liberate your consciousness from the chains that connect you to the other "selves" that are still vibrating under the influence of the lower spheres of their egos. This will break the cycle of reincarnation, or Samsara Wheel.

This creates a vortex of "enlightenment," so to speak, that will influence, illuminate, and help all the other selves to also break free from their repetitive cycle.

It's a force that can open the doors of freedom but depends on the level of awareness and spiritual evolution of each one of them at that time, that will allow them to pass through the eye of the needle and take the quantum leap to liberation.

All of the mind stretching exercises or illuminating insights that we can have about what happens after the liberation are obviously an unknown ground for those who didn't achieve that state yet, but the most important thing to realize now is that ego generates karma, and that duality and fragmentation are the blockages that prevent us from achieving our ultimate freedom.

If you become the master of your ego, you will instantly see yourself as one with others and merge with all aspects of creation. In that state of oneness, it will be impossible to be fooled by duality and separation, it will be impossible to "sin," because your consciousness will be integrated with the whole creation, therefore, impossible to create karma. You will be free.

═══ CHAPTER 17 ═══

REINCARNATION
AND AFTERLIFE

The phenomenon of near-death experience was exhaustively studied by many doctors, hypnotists, scientists, and spiritual teachers. It's interesting to note that in practically all the cases, the "clinically dead" persons describe almost identical experiences after they return to life.

They all say that at the moment of their death, they find themselves in a body of light and meet beloved dead relatives, guides, angels, or a light being that fits the soul's religious beliefs.

They are there to greet the soul and escort her through a tunnel of light that leads to a sort of afterlife realm.

The beings of light seem to act as the soul's guardians and mentors and are there to give comfort and guidance in the soul's journey to the spiritual plane.

After having spent some time with her discarnate beloveds, in bliss and awe, feeling a sense of freedom and indescribable love, the soul is presented with a "Life Review," which is a holographic movie of her entire life.

Every single experience, from birth to death, is watched and relived by the soul that can see clearly all the situations in which she failed and sinned. She realizes all the things that she could have done better and regrets.

Amongst all the reported cases, just few of them get to the point of the life review experience. Most are sent back to earth by a light being, a

Jesus, or simply a voice that tells the soul that she can't stay there because it's not her time yet.

Such experiences are also confirmed by discarnate entities that communicate with incarnate "mediums." These ones were able to explain what happens on the other side, even further, after the life review.

The usual story is that, after the life review, the soul agrees that the best thing to do is to reincarnate on earth again, usually with the same group of people, to have the opportunity to fix all her mistakes. This time, the soul prepares all the scenario, challenges, and situations that would be favorable to the success of her mission. Some souls are allowed to stay longer to heal and recover from their traumas, until they are ready for their next "round" on earth.

All the soul's memories are erased at the time they are sent into a new body. She dives into a dark womb, and from this point on, her new adventure begins.

The soul is told if she is successful in her planned journey, burns all the karmas, learns her lessons, changes and evolves, she will be allowed to graduate and ascend to the next level, where reincarnation on earth is just an option, because many other experiences in higher planes can also be available for her.

I have absolutely no question about the legitimacy of these testimonies. It seems clear to me that all these people really lived such experiences. However, I can't help but have so many questions about this pre-organized spiritual system, in the astral. Certain things seem a little awkward and suspicious to me.

It's understandable and even acceptable that most souls need guidance and help on the other side, and this might be even necessary for a soul who is lost and not able to navigate such intricate astral plane. Some people even die in violent or traumatic ways and finding themselves out of their physical bodies in an unknown territory must be very disorienting.

I also believe that there are angels and guides that are higher expressions of ourselves ready to assist us in our evolutionary process. However, my questions are—

Why practically all souls find themselves in such a disempowering position when they die?

Why the result of all life reviews leads the soul to the reincarnation process? With amnesia and unable to remember her past mistakes, what chances will the soul have to make all things right next time?

Why all the scenarios and everything that's construed in this between-lives area are a perfect replica of the soul's best dreams and beliefs?

Why all the experiences prepared for the soul seem to suggest that the best option is reincarnation?

It's a fact that there are inter-dimensional beings that can shape-shift into any form they want. They have also access to the Akashic Records of any individual and are able to play life reviews easily to unsuspecting naïve souls that are craving for help and ready to accept any guidance.

They are masters in trickery and can mimic anything they wish. They are technologically extremely advanced but parasitic in nature. Is it possible that some of the lost, and disoriented souls might be deceived by such shape-shifting entities and persuaded to reincarnate in endless cycles, so that these entities can feed off their energy?

Since we are creative beings, we can project in the astral everything we desire. If we die and believe in Jesus, it's Jesus that we will find on the other side. If we believe in Shiva, we will find him there; if we expect to see a beloved dead relative, he will be there waiting for us with open arms.

Is that possible that our creative abilities can be manipulated to make us believe that what we see is real?

My point is … anything is possible if you are not grounded in your sovereign space. The astral is not that different from here; it's just made of a subtler, lighter, and more pliable energy.

Yes, I know for a fact that archangels, angels, ascended masters, and guides are the most divine expressions of God's love, and they are always there for us when needed.

I also believe in their magnificence, and by being pure unconditional love, any help they would want to give us in the spiritual realms would certainly be towards EMPOWERMENT and FREEDOM.

They should want us to be the ones to graduate ourselves if our vibration is high enough to embody sovereignty. They should want us to be the ones to decide where to go, what to create, and with whom we would want to share our energy.

Our vibrational frequency should be the ONLY factor to determine what dimensional realm belongs to us. We should know that and expect nothing less.

The problem is that we were bred to feel helpless and beg for a SAVIOR. We are always waiting for someone or anything external to us to save us. Jesus will save us and come rescue us in a cloud of glory; I don't need to move a finger. All I need to do is believe. Our favorite benevolent extraterrestrial race will be there, when the trumpets sound, to rescue us. Really?

The "savior complex" is imbued in the core of our being, a program so brilliantly crafted in our DNA that became part of us.

All our relationships are based on "need" and who will save who.

In our lowest moments, what do we do? We wait for someone to "save" us. Religious beliefs are all founded in the savior mentality and the cultivation of crippling disempowering beliefs.

If we die and go to the other side expecting a savior, we will certainly find it. But watch out, because it might not be exactly what you expect, and the price to pay might be too high.

WE ARE OUR SAVIORS AND THE ONES WE ARE WAITING FOR.

Jesus came here in this dark place to show us by example how to ascend, how to find CHRIST, the perfect divine man inside us, how to transcend any mundane limitations and embrace our divinity. He came here to show us that we can be like Him that we are gods with amnesia, and that all we need to do is REMEMBER.

This is not arrogance nor a pretentious statement.

Everybody needs help at any given moment of their lives, and they should certainly look for the appropriate help when needed. But the point is that we should use any help to empower and enable us to do our part in the game of life, not waiting for a savior to rescue us, like powerless victims.

I want to close this chapter with a very important tip:

At the moment of our death, a gigantic portal is open for us.

This is a tremendous opportunity for us to jump into any alternate reality we want. All we need to do is set our intention and focus our point of attention into merging with our higher self.

Don't think about who or what you are leaving behind.

Worries or attachments with earthly matters will pull your spirit down into the between-lives area, in the astral. Be aware that you can be free and that the lower realms are INSIDE the higher ones. You will not abandon any beloved one if you jump into a higher dimension when you die. You will just be in a position of reaching them out from a higher plane of existence. You can become an angel to them and assist them from a tremendously powerful place. But at the instant of your death, you must be detached from everything. All parts of your spirit must be concentrated on this "jump."

Our higher self is our Christ Self, the expression of our highest potential. If we can merge with it, we'll be embodying human divinity in its highest form.

The sages know that at the moment of death, whatever it's in our minds is what we are going to attract.

They know that a dimensional portal is open, and we can jump dimensions; we can give a quantum leap into divine realms.

All we need to do is understand that we can bypass the lower realms and be one with our higher self.

Be courageous and see your individual sparkle of light merging with the grandiosity of your higher self at the moment of your last breath and embrace freedom.

Before I close this chapter, I would like to invite you to adventure into some mind stretching "out of the box" possibilities for the theme reincarnation, that are not based on linear concepts.

If you admit the possibility of a holographic multidimensional universe, in which space and time is a by-product of human creation, it's not implausible to also accept the idea that there are many aspects of yourself incarnating and experiencing their lives simultaneously, along multiple timelines … Example: Mary being born in 1502, Peter in 1830, Joe in 1920, Carl in 2090 (the future), you in 1990, and so forth.

All of them having a unique ego and a separate individuality but interconnected by the same "Mother Energy" and the same frequency signature, so to speak, since all of them come from the same collective consciousness called higher self.

Therefore, you can say that Mary, Peter, and Joe are your DIFFERENT past lives "selves" and that Carl is your DIFFERENT future life "self" because each ego-complex is different from each other.

And from the perspective of your higher self, he/she can say that all of you are IDENTICAL parts of him or her, because the higher self is the sum of all the "selves" together.

I call these simultaneous space-time incarnations HORIZONTAL incarnations.

Now...the science of quantum physics talks a lot about reversing time or time folding itself backwards.

Therefore, it's not far-fetched that every single "self" can repeat himself/herself back in time as many times as they want, to live the same life over and over, in order to perfect a single life scenario reality.

I call this reincarnation scenario VERTICAL incarnations.

Can you see how wide are the possibilities for the higher self to play endlessly with all alternate possibilities?

And I am not even talking about the pieces of the higher self that are incarnating in other planets or dimensions.

This might sound like fiction to many, but I tell you that sometimes fiction movies are perhaps much closer to the truth than the 3D constricted reality we live in.

If you are a "graduated" evolved soul, by merging with your higher self you can acquire the ability to nano travel anywhere you want, in any dimension of any realm you desire.

You can time jump multidimensionally, live one reality at a time or multiple at the same time, as it pleases, just by focusing your point of attention into one or many nexus points in the quantum field.

This also gives you a pale idea on how advanced are the consciousness of certain galactic races, travelers of the Universe. We have been visited by extremely evolved "future versions of ourselves" since the beginning of our civilization.

Some of them are even walking among us, undetected.

The concept of "multiple versions of earth" existing in many different dimensions (3D, 4D, 5D) is not far-fetched either.

As we expand our consciousness, we begin to experience higher, brighter, and happier versions of earth.

Even if we are witnessing tremendous chaos around us in 3D, that chaotic reality is not "touching" us. Our consciousness is separate from it like a glass wall, and we are not being affected by it because our frequency is higher and much more compatible with a higher vibratory dimensional reality.

That's why Jesus used the expression: "Living in the world without belonging to it."

CHAPTER 18

THE MATRIX

I suppose almost everybody has already watched the movie "The Matrix" with Keanu Reeves. If you haven't, I strongly recommend you do.

I can say this movie could be a documentary because it shows brilliantly how the matrix of the earth has been highjacked, how we mistake illusion for reality, and how we walk around like sleeping zombies, devoid of any awareness of the deeper levels of manipulation and deceit we have been subjected to. In other words, we have been taking the blue pill for thousands and thousands of years.

The red pill represents the human awakening and the perception of reality without the glasses of illusion.

The outer energetic atmosphere of the earth is a soup of frequencies created by the collective vibrations of humanity, the vibrations of the elements of nature, and the electromagnetic field spectrum of the planet called Schumann Resonance.

Such resonances are generated and stimulated by lightning discharges in the cavity formed by the earth's surface and the ionosphere. It's a fact that the Schumann Resonance of the earth is increasing rapidly in the last few years. This is one of the signs that our planet is going through a tremendous planetary shift that will affect all humanity.

Gaia, or Mother Earth, is a living, intelligent, and sentient entity and so are all the planets, suns, and stars. Therefore, in a way, the collective of humanity forms the oversoul of earth.

Whoever lives a very artificial life, disconnected from nature and its elements, is detached from a tremendous source of spiritual energy.

The intricate network of life is like a spiderweb where all is interdependent and vibrates in unison.

The vital energy emanated by humans is also known as "lush."

Our planetary grid is then formed by the conjunction of all these frequencies together.

The earth's magnetosphere has two belts known as Van Allen Radiation Belt, which is a zone of energetic charged particles, most of which originate from the solar wind that is captured by and held around the earth.

It's important to remember that the frequencies we radiate are generated by our thoughts, ideas, emotions, and actions. All these vibrations are, for lack of better words, "floating" in the vibratory field of the earth and contribute enormously to the formation of the matrix.

This grid is known in the spiritual communities as "matrix", a word that denotes "maya," the world of illusions, like in the movie "The Matrix". This concept is used to denote an artificial construct created by the manipulation of natural organic etheric substances to purposely highjack the collective planetary consciousness.

This grid limits the individual to a very narrow frequency band and prevents the earthlings from exiting the earth's etheric confines and some inter-dimensional beings from entering it.

Some authors that have researched this subject in depth say that our natural matrix that was created to hold the 3D construct together was highjacked, as I mentioned before, by some technologically highly advanced but very negative inter-dimensional galactic races that created an artificial matrix on the top of the previous "organic" one. This was possible mainly by heavily influencing our perceptions, thoughts, and beliefs through multiple means of mind control programs in addition to technological manipulation of certain frequencies.

It's irrelevant if you believe in this version or not, because the most important thing to do is to admit our willing participation in this "crime," take ownership of our actions, and hold the sword of liberation towards freedom. There are no dark forces that can stand a warrior of light that's aware of his power.

The term matrix implies the idea that we, humans, are captive of a grid of illusions in which falsehood and deceit is used as a weapon against us to subdue humanity and extract our "lush". The agenda is to continue holding together the matrix of false belief systems permanently.

The only way to destroy the matrix walls is to stop projecting limiting thought forms into the grid.

If we could see clearly how our energy is being harvested and used for our own enslavement, that awareness would be like a missile launched against this prison, and not one single brick of this illusory wall of deception would stand.

We are in 2021 now, as I write these words, and due to the present chaotic crisis, more and more people are awakening, and as this number continues to grow, a great part of humanity will step out of the prison of their minds and choose wiser and better timelines for themselves and for the planet.

The parasitic opportunistic tentacles of these controlling forces can and should be removed and they must starve to death, since we have been their food source for thousands of years.

Every person that wakes up, steps into his/her sovereign space, and stops complying with this dark agenda is a stone thrown against the matrix's walls.

The more people awaken, the more holes are made in the matrix's walls until a critical mass of people is achieved to bring it to the ground.

It all begins with our own inner walls of deception. As I said many times, if there is no prey, no predator will appear.

If the matrix collapses, there will be a rip in the veil that holds our old perceptions together, and our consciousness will begin to merge with the fourth and fifth dimensional astral planes.

Our constricted perception of reality will expand into a broader spectrum. Some of us will be able to reach the 5D level; others will remain in the higher layers of the 4D plane.

The ones who are strongly attached to old beliefs, heavy vibrations of attachments, resentment, denial, fear, victimhood, anger, violence, and judgement will be integrated into a compatible parallel construct by vibrational match.

If an individual's light quotient is not high enough to hold higher frequencies, the universe finds a way to rearrange everything and place each piece of the puzzle where it belongs.

There is an overwhelming material about the negative inter-dimensional races, the "Fallen Angels," the false gods, and their human bloodlines puppets, known as the "Illuminati," that hold positions of power in all areas of our society.

It's believed that these bloodline families are responsible for terrible crimes against humanity for centuries. They hide themselves behind the deeper layers of religions, ritualistic satanic cults like the Masonry, the Jesuits, and the Vatican, believe me or not.

These researchers are called "conspiracy theorists." They have been attacked and ridiculed for centuries.

This sounds like a horror movie, but after I researched long enough, after I read many whistle blowers' materials, heard uncountable witnesses and victims of their horrible deeds, I am fully convinced that most conspiracy theorists are telling the truth.

Most of them spent their entire lives with no material gain, risking their lives, suffering all sorts of threats, some had members of their families killed … all to try to help and awaken humanity.

It seems that now we are living in a dark age in which the grip of evil is tight because they know the veil is thinning and their horrific plans are being debunked by some.

The so-called "New World Order," that's about to be implemented, clearly has an agenda of centralization of power, domination, and totalitarian control of the whole human race.

The "GREAT RESET" is about transferring global wealth and ownership rights to the technocratic elite and giving them the power to control the world's nations.

Here are some of the Great Reset platforms:

- Depopulation agenda through the bio-engineered coronavirus, aiming to target mainly the elders, who are a financial drain to the government, the weak, and the frail.
- The same hand that created the problem came with the solution: A deadly and crippling genetic experimental "vaccine," never tried in humans before. This will of course take care of the rest, and the ones who survive can be infertile. So far, after just three months of vaccination, more people were killed and permanently injured

than the sum of fifteen years of all vaccines together. By the way, these are not my words; it's the CDC official data. It's there for all to see.

- Using FEAR as a weapon against the populace, to induce them to comply, obey, and even beg for masks, lockdowns, and the "miracle shots."

- Promoting division, separation, and isolation with forced lockdowns. If you break UNITY, you fragment and deactivate people's ability of discernment, making them more prone to compliance. The index of suicide since lockdowns were implemented is alarming, especially among teenagers ... But of course, if everybody takes the jab, all will return to "normal" and life will be great again.

- Vaccine Passports: If you don't have one, no permission to travel or enter any establishment, no schools for your kids, no entertainment, no work, no life. This is ingeniously linked to a credit score system that will classify everyone according to his/her level of obedience.

- The installation of 5G towers in the entire planetary grid to back up the "transhumanism" agenda, the Machine kingdom.

- Artificial intelligence taking most human jobs, causing constant and growing waves of Unemployment.

- Universal Basic Income: The worse form of communism. Goodbye small business, goodbye economic freedom, goodbye dreams.

- Gender Indoctrination: Children will be "educated" to choose what gender they want to embrace. Boy or girl? Very efficient as a population reduction tactic.
The feminization of man and masculinization of woman. The destruction of family values and the demoralization of sex.

- Intentional decimation of the global economy and the old way of life, thereby justifying the Great Reset.

- Elimination of the fiat dollar and the implementation of digital currency. A preparation for total financial control.

- ID 2020: The "Mark of the Beast." The insertion of an electromagnetic chip under the human skin. Nothing can be bought or sold without it. The nanobots in the mRNA vaccines are already part of this agenda.

- Massive A.I. surveillance: If you are a bad boy, or girl, your "privileges" will be cut. The all-seeing eye will put you in jail or remove your citizens' rights (if any is left.
- The centralization of the population into smart cities for better control and AI surveillance.
- The crushing of all farmers' abilities to produce food.
- The takeover and control of all farmlands to hold the food production monopoly. Whoever controls food, controls the world.
- Elimination of All Fossil Fuel: All will be electric. Everything will depend on the grid. In case of an EMF attack or if the electric grid collapses, no food, no heat, no transportation, no survival.
- No more private property. "You will owe nothing, and you will be happy." A brilliantly designed plan to transfer wealth from everything and everyone into the hands of the controllers. They play the music, we dance.

This seems to me like the worse form of totalitarianism that makes Venezuela look like heaven on earth.

If you think this is exaggeration or conspiracy paranoia, think again, research, and look around. It's happening right now, in plain sight, but most are too busy, too brainwashed or too scared to even question anything. They just want their lives to come back to "normal" and return to their ordinary mundane affairs.

The truth is, our world is run by satanic criminal psychopaths, and if we sit and do nothing about it, they will have our "power of attorney" to implement every single one of these measures and we will have no rights to complain or blame anyone for our enslavement.

How could we get to this point?

The answer is ACQUIESCENCE.

The frog is put into a pot full of water. When the temperature gradually increases, it doesn't notice until it's too late to jump out of the boiling water.

I hope in my heart that at the time my grandkids read this book, they will be doing so from a great place. I hope our future generations will be able to escape the indoctrination of such reductionist limiting education system and will have the chance to build a better world for all.

I hope they will be able to balance technology with the natural organic way of living, integrated with nature and all living things, instead of being enslaved by artificial intelligence and becoming soulless bio-robots with marionette strings attached to their limbs.

I hope they will become the light warriors of this beautiful planet and the guardians of our sacred living library.

And I hope they can understand the lessons of love, compassion, and equality and be the bringers of liberation to our entire race.

At this moment, we are in a bifurcation of timelines, and the choices we make now will determine the future of humanity.

There are amazing possibilities for our future, waiting for us to awaken and reclaim our real place in the universe.

I pray that at least a critical mass of people will be able to see the BIG PICTURE and use this nexus point to jump into a fifth dimensional timeline, joining Gaia in her planetary ascension to higher and happier realms.

I believe that wherever there's evil, there's also goodness.

The pendular movement of duality, after reaching its extreme point, must bounce back to the other side.

The extreme nexus point is now. And it's up to us to make it bounce back full force with the power of our conscious choices.

CHAPTER 19

ASCENSION DEMYSTIFIED

Ascension is the most used term in the modern new age spiritual movement nowadays, but this concept is biblically ancient. It's mentioned in the scriptures as "rapture," and many ancient texts describe the process of the evolution of the human soul through self-actualization and gradual spiritual elevation until she is able to ascend to higher levels of consciousness

I mention below a very summarized description of the three first stages of the soul ascension from our physical 3D consciousness until it reaches the fifth dimension.

It would be useless to go further, since when a person reaches 5D, everything illuminates in such a way that all realities are seen through a much broader perspective, through the eyes of the spirit. Below there is a brief summary of the traits of a person who ascends from one dimension to another:

3rd density existence – Body Consciousness – Physicality

The person is driven by the lower aspects of consciousness, conditional love, divisive, actions based on fear, lack of compassion or empathy, judging others and self, competitive, self-righteous, identifies with physical body, self-indulgence, self-importance, arrogance, controlled by the lower chakras, animal sex, world of scarcity, needy, self-destructive, prone to physical and emotional addictions, controlling, insecure, fight-or-flight response to stimulus, emotionally charged by past and future, guilt and shame, victimhood, lack of self-esteem.

4th density existence – Astral/Emotional Body – Astral Plane

Transition from ego fear-based reality to love, spiritual awakening, consciousness expansion, purging of negative emotions and belief systems, realizing self is not a body, physical/energetic changes, tap into collective consciousness, increased telepathy, out-of-body experiences, thinning of the veil, realization that something is changing in the world.

5th density existence – Mental Light Body – Mental Plan

Egoless, self-love, service to others, actions based on unconditional love, ongoing gratitude, self-realized, fearless, no limits, less dense body, unity-minded, recognizes self as part of the whole, easy manifestation, goes with the flow, duality and linear time dissolves, the only time is now, no need for possessions or status.

Usually, people ascend in "layers depending on their different degrees of consciousness and their unique individual process.

Many of us bounce from one phase to another until the "zero point" of balance is reached and a quantum leap is done towards freedom and enlightenment. For more clarity, let me divide the phases into five categories according to their level of evolution, also keeping in mind that there's an invisible line from which people transition from phase to phase until the alchemy of purification is completed. This is an endless process and there are no limits for the soul's evolution.

1. The 3D Sleep Slumbers: There are those who are not able to ascend in this present "great awakening wave" because they are deeply ingrained in the falsehood and deceit of the matrix game.

    Their beliefs and actions are cemented in their five physical senses.
    They are not interested, totally reject, or even ridicule any idea that doesn't fit into their crystallized 3D perceptions.
    They pursue only material things and earthly pleasures as means of happiness and fulfillment.

2. The Searchers: In this category are those who began to sense that there is something more to life than just the pursuit of survival and material conquests.

They begin to search for answers and are open to the unknown. They become curious and begin to question the meaning of life yet heavily influenced by the matrix system.

3. The Warriors: Those are the brilliant minds of all researchers and brave warriors, who risk and dedicate their lives in the process of unmasking and debunking the matrix game, its players, their agendas and manipulations.

    The more radical ones are called "conspiracy theorists."
    For the most part, their goal is to open humanity's eyes and empower each individual to break free from the abuse and domination that happen in our 3D world.
    Some are even able to go beyond the 3D and 4D perceptions and explore aspects of the "domino effect" multidimensionally.
    However, the gravitational pull of the focus of their attention is so ingrained in the duality of what happens here that their consciousness is mostly anchored in the lower dimensions.

4. The Dreamers: In this category are those who know how everything works in 3D illusion and realize that by the law of attraction and by raising their vibrations to a higher frequency, they will be aligned with a much more positive timeline.

    They discovered one of the most important secrets of all: ENERGY FLOWS WHERE ATTENTION GOES.
    However, some refuse to hear, feel, or act upon anything that is not "Love and Light," pushing away everything else that's not a vibrational match to the higher spheres.
    Some of them even fall into the trap of judgement and separation, by repelling other people's ideas, especially those of category 3, as if they would contaminate their "immaculate auras" with negativity.
    They remain inside their spiritual bubbles no matter what happens in the physical reality.
    Unfortunately, WHAT YOU RESIST PERSISTS, so duality is there as well.

5. The Masters: These true teachers are the rare individuals whose consciousness encompasses all categories in a space of love, compassion, and a higher understanding.

    They see the BIG PICTURE from a multidimensional perspective, therefore, with NO JUDGEMENT.
    They know it's all part of themselves; hence, they become immune to negativity as we perceive it. Their magnetic aura radiates the pure light of love and compassion to the whole world, inspiring and uplifting others and leading by example.
    They courageously dive into darkness when needed and rise to heavens with humility, alchemically transforming the dark into light.
    Immortality is achieved even when inside their physical bodies; they overcome duality not by battling the opposite polarities but integrating them into a higher understanding.
    They embody the divine will and their lives are dedicated to serve and help the evolution of humanity, the planet, and the universe.

If you are a positively polarized person, who has a pure heart, a burning desire to better yourself and help others, integrate with nature, is sensitive to worldly causes, and if your sense of justice is based on mercy, compassion, and forgiveness, you are already far in your ascension path.

You don't need to be a vegan, meditate endless hours in isolation, or resign the pleasures of the world to be a spiritual person.

On the contrary, we have a physical body and live in a material world of polarities and extreme duality for a reason.

Friction and struggles are a big part of our learning process.

The world of actions is a platform designed to propel the soul towards growth and elevation.

We are here to embody spirit into matter and bring redemption into this dark place.

Each one of us has a unique frequency signature, unique gifts and traits specifically crafted by the Creator's hands. No one is exactly like you, and no one can manifest things the way you do.

That's why you are so important and so special. Love your uniqueness and explore your talents in a way that will bring you joy and fulfillment, and as a by-product, illuminate others.

You are called and descended into this dark realm to shine the light that no one else can shine.

Humanity is a mosaic made of individual precious stones, each one with a different color, brilliance, and beauty. If just one of them is missing, the artwork is incomplete.

Your first mission on this planet is to be AUTHENTIC, to love who you are and radiate this love in everything you do and every person you touch. This is ascension.

CHAPTER 20

ANGELS, GUIDES, AND MEDIUMSHIP

We all have guides that assist us in our evolution process.

Some are with us since birth; others appear in certain phases of our life to assist us in the things that require an expertise that will be helpful in each specific situation.

These guides gain their personal expansion through helping and learning from another being's physical experiences.

So, it's a mutual symbiosis, since by being in the spiritual realm, their perspectives are a little broader than ours.

The guides that you are experiencing right now are a match to your energetic vibration. When you set up the intention for your future life, before birth, the guides that will be chosen by mutual agreement will be the ones who are interested in living the same kind of experiences as you are but don't necessarily want to incarnate in physicality.

So, we can say that your guides are discarnate friends who are there to help you to stay aligned with your original intention, and by doing so, they will also learn, grow, and evolve with you. A perfect situation, beneficial for both parties.

There are no divisions or classifications in the spiritual world, however, for a better understanding, I will mention the main basic types of guides, based on their level of evolution and the spiritual light they hold:

The first kind are called LIGHT BODY. These are the angels and ascended masters.

They have an incredibly high vibratory rate, so they are perceived as pure light.

Most likely, they assist those whose life work is aligned with higher spiritual planes, like healers and spiritual teachers. Because they are not limited by space and time, their focus of attention can split into multiple realms simultaneously, and by being from the seventh to eleventh dimensional planes, they are able to assist many people at the same time.

The second type of guides are the ARCHETYPAL GUIDES. They are symbolic representatives of the way they used to appear in their previous lives, like the magician, the healer, the warrior, etc. They are a match to your intentions.

As every thought that ever existed is available in the eternal now moment, the thought of the identity that they used to have in their past lives can be reactivated by Source Energy for your understanding in this life, because they have a symbolic meaning to you.

It's interesting to note that as your vibration shifts to a higher rate, and as your intentions get more expanded, a new set of guides who match your new evolutionary level will be assigned to you.

The third type of guide is what we call ANCESTRAL GUIDES... These are the ones who are related to us through our physical lineage: grandfather, great-grandmother, mother, brother, sister, etc.

The fourth kind is the ANIMAL GUIDE. It could be a deceased pet that you had in your physical life, but most likely they are what the native Americans call a totem.

When certain tribes shape-shift into an animal totem, that means that they were taking on the vibratory rate of that animal that they relate to.

Now, the most important of all guides is your HIGHER SELF. the energy of your eternal self projecting itself through your physical body. It's the spirit guide that you are the expression of.

The spirit guides can help you with many things in your life: arrange synchronicities, intensify intuitions, facilitate encounters with people, help with healing if invited, help you to keep going towards your desired goals and align them to your highest purposes.

It's important to understand that guides cannot interfere with your free will. They come when invited and help you when needed but never infringing the universal law of free will. So it's important that you make them part of your free will and ask for them if you want them to be part of your life.

Now, how can you communicate with your spirit guides?

When you create a thought, that thought is translated into energy that can be received and understood by your guides, angels, masters, higher self, God, or anything that has consciousness. It's only in your physical life that you separate thinking from communication, so they will respond energetically the same way. It's like a radio dial tuned into a frequency.

Communication with your spirit guides is all about RAISING YOUR FREQUENCY to the wavelength they can perceive.

Step number 1 is to set your intention. Intentions are powerful.

Their response will come through the most open venue that you have. Not everyone perceives what we call "beyond the senses" information the same way.

We have clairvoyance (receiving mental pictures), clairaudience (hearing with your extra-senses), physical intuition (perceiving energies with our bodies), emotional intuition (empaths, perceives with their heart chakra, or emotional center), and spiritual intuition (sense of just knowing).

So, your guides will talk to you through your most open channel, then the information goes to the second strongest type, and so on, as you keep opening your intuitive centers.

Meditations, rituals, and breath work help the brain to stop interfering with resisting thoughts, like making you doubt if what you are broadcasting is real.

In meditation, try to find that space between thoughts, that stillness, watching your breath and patiently bringing your thoughts back to the breath with no judgement. Find your inner silence and begin to feel your vibratory field expanding.

When you find yourself in this quiet space, you can ask your guides to identify themselves to you.

The principal guide is the one who is with you most of the time; this is the one that usually approaches you first.

Try to identify what sensations each of your guides have on your emotions or your body. That energy signature will help you to identify which one is communicating with you.

The most important thing is to put your mind to rest, in a total state of receptivity, and trust what comes next.

There is no one venue in which the information can be presented to you. It could be through symbols, names, sentences, images, or symbolic signs. Guides translate the information into your "hard drive" in ways that you will be able to understand better, depending on how your brain is "wired" and on your belief systems.

Automatic writing is another way to channel your guides, especially if you are a physical channeler.

You can get a piece of paper and write down whatever questions you have to your guides, without any judgement or expectation in your mind, and start to write the answers you sense, feel, or hear.

Another way is out-of-body experiences or lucid dreaming. You can encounter them very quickly with this method. They will be right there waiting for you and it's very easy to feel their presence.

It's very rewarding to realize that you are never alone and that there's an army of light beings that you can count on at every moment of your life. Invite them to participate in your creation.

You will be amazed on how gratifying it is to be able to count on such precious help at any moment of your life.

Our guides are magical energetic expressions of our own consciousness, magnified in higher individual signatures.

They are part of a multifaceted stream of energy from which you are also part of but on the other end of the spectrum.

Explore this gift in awe and gratitude.

Before trying to communicate with your guides, a good piece of advice would be to stay away from alcohol, drugs, or any toxic substances that can interfere with the purity of your body, before you invite them into your space.

Channeling is a beautiful and very uplifting thing, but it could be also dangerous if your "filter" is dirty or contaminated.

The higher you elevate your vibrations, the better your "radio reception" will be, so to speak, and the safer the experience.

The last thing you want is to call Batman and get the Joker from the other side.

CHAPTER 21

THE ART OF RELATIONSHIPS

The main reason why we chose to come here in this 3D playground of souls is to have experiences that will help us learn, grow, and expand our consciousness.

Finding joy and fulfillment while playing the game of life is the art of living.

Relationships are mirrors that reflect our own image. We find ourselves in others, and we see our light and our darkness in every single individual we encounter in life.

The symbol of the cross, two lines, one horizontal, the other vertical, intersecting each other in the middle, also represents the mundane and the divine parts of men.

If we are not able to find God horizontally, in others, we will never find Him vertically.

When we sever our connection with the spirit, we block the flow of the divine nectar that nourishes us with pure love. We become empty, dry, and unable to channel this loving energy to anyone. That's what I call "EXISTENTIAL VOID."

But we are still hungry, empty, and needy, so what do we do?

We automatically look to quench our thirst through others.

And this is the base for almost all relationships in the world.

In this unconscious process, we become parasitic, ego-centered, and needy. The other is there to give us what we need, to correspond our expectations, and to nourish us with the energy we need to exist.

When our partner does not fulfill this role, we get disappointed, frustrated, enraged, or depressed.

When we say, "You disappointed me," that means "I expected certain things from you, and you failed to correspond. If you don't give me what I want, I will find someone else who can."

It's very common to hear people saying, "I didn't think he/she was like that. At the beginning, he/she was different."

So, what's the problem?

The problem is that many people doesn't know how to draw energy from the never-ending Source.

Their connection with the universe is blocked, because of their identification with the EGO. And when the ego rules, the relationship is doomed.

What we see in most relationships is mutual vampirism, parasitism, the infatuation of superficial aspects, such as looks and material possessions, and the allurement of the enchanting spells of the physical senses. And we call this love.

When we say, "I love you," that means "I need you." But we think we are giving our best to our partner, while we can't give anything if we have nothing to give.

So, just a small part of us is putting itself in the relationship: the ego. The rest is dormant and unconscious. Thus, the most precious part of us is forgotten and neglected. And this is exactly the part that will bring us happiness, the part that knows how to love.

Every person that crosses our path, that we relate with, is there to show us something. Sometimes a part of us that we are avoiding facing, sometimes certain aspects of ourselves that we need to work on, or attachments that we must let go of.

All we need to do is to have the courage to look at the reflection of the mirror in the eyes of the other person and see our image in it and the things we need to learn about ourselves.

But some people may say, "But I had an abusive spouse, and I am not abusive at all."

Of course, you are not. You are just his counterpart. You are the submissive, the compliant, the lack of self-esteem, the subservient, the victim, and the poor sense of self-worth that ATTRACTED him. He would not be in your movie if you had not invited him as the main actor.

So, sometimes, the mirror reflection is identical, and sometimes is the opposite. But both are there to show you something.

A very extreme example of this syndrome is the condition called NARCISSISM.

In psychology, the definition of narcissism is—

"A mental condition in which people have an inflated sense of their own importance, a deep need for excessive attention and admiration, troubled relationships, and a lack of empathy for others." But behind this mask of extreme confidence lies a fragile self-esteem that's vulnerable to the slightest criticism.

A full-blown narcissist is a huge blackhole that sucks in and destroys everything and everyone that's on its path.

Some spiritual teachers even dare to say that a narcissist's soul is permanently lost or he never had one. In the latter case, they use the expression "organic portals," which means they have a bio-suit called physical body, but the divine sparkle of light is not there or it's long gone.

We all carry some narcissistic traits, which is acceptable, but some people can fit 100 percent in this category.

If you happen to come across a full-blown narcissist, these are what you will find:

- They are always right; you are always wrong.
- They never listen and are not interested in what you say.
- My way or no way.
- They know everything, you know nothing.
- They always pull you down and belittle you.
- They are extremely selfish and vain.
- They are extremely manipulative, arrogant and self-centered.
- They always use others for their own gain.
- They don't know how to share.
- They want to dominate and possess.
- They gaslight you all the time.
- They project their faults on you.
- They accuse, judge, and diminish you in everything.

- They make you believe you need them for everything.
- They are control freaks.
- They are mentally, emotionally, and/or physically abusive.
- They lack compassion and empathy. Sometimes they mimic such feelings but there are no genuine feelings inside.
- You are always guilty of anything that doesn't work as they expect.

So, if you happen to find one in your path, RUN!

I know it doesn't sound like a very spiritual thing to say, but it's the most spiritual thing you can ever do in your life, to be honest.

More precisely, spiritual self-preservation and an action of self-respect.

One of the most misunderstood aspects of the word "love" is the assumption that we always have to give, forgive everything, and "give the other cheek," overlooking all the faults and negative actions of the person we love.

Women, specially, tend to give endlessly, even when the other does absolutely nothing to earn it. Mothers do that every time.

This is called "THE BREAD OF SHAME."

I came from a family in which our mothers, grandmothers, and great-grandmothers were the epiphany of the self-sacrifice on behalf of their offspring. They all were wonderful mothers but were unknowingly teaching their kids how to be a martyr and how to disown and neglect their own royalty.

When you are possessed by the bread of shame syndrome, a very precious part of you is given to the other in exchange for a sense of validation and self-worth.

A mother would never be a good mother if she is self-centered and egotistic but taking things to the other extreme is also a way of negating self-love. The same also applies to all relationships.

Balance and healthy boundaries are the two main ingredients for a healthy and long-lasting relationship. If the pendulum goes too much to one side or another, the structure crumbles.

One of the big mistakes we make in relationships is to invest all we have, expecting that the other person will change.

Most of the time our ego doesn't want to let go of certain addictions; for instance, something that your partner is giving you that "you can't live without" (chemistry is a great example) that makes us overlook everything else.

A significant amount of people gets so obsessed and attached to the object of their desires that they keep putting all the cards in a game that was already lost long time ago. They don't want to admit that "it's as good as it gets" and keep feeding the hopes that the other person will change. I think it's where the expression "love is blind" comes from. It would be more accurate to say, "ego is blind."

Be also mindful if you engage in a relationship with an addict of any sort, severe bipolar, or if you are the one who has this dependency.

I already explained what alcoholism and drugs do to your body, mind, and spirit.

There are plenty of materials that teach how to recover from addictions and how to deal with beloveds that are addicts. I don't want to go into these details here. But if you feel a repetitive pattern of engaging with addicts, there might be aspects of you that are there to sabotage and prevent you from choosing healthier and more uplifting relationships. In this case, it would be advisable to look for professional help while also finding ways to heal your spirit.

It would be unfair to put all the cases in a single basket and generalize. There are alcoholics, addicts, severe bipolar individuals, and many other souls that face horrible obstacles that find the inner strength to look for help and consistently persist in their healing process. Many successful stories are a light at the end of the tunnel and an inspiration for many.

However, if your beloveds refuse to admit they need help, if they deny healing, they will be digging a hole in their own boats. So, the best thing to do is to leave the boat before it sinks.

Everyone is responsible for their destiny and the choices are individual. If you insist on keeping any drama in your life, you will be karmically responsible for the choices you make.

Now, more than ever, it's time to let go of all unnecessary negative burdens that hold us down and move forward in our ascension path. The universe will then conspire to align us with the right people that will add forces to ours, instead of constantly draining them.

The ideal love relationship is the one in which both give with no bargain and no previous expectations, both are able to see the beauty and magnificence of their counterparts, both are aligned in similar and complimentary goals and aspirations, where there is mutual trust, where the individualities and differences are respected and appreciated, where there's patience, tolerance, kindness, mutual care, and positive complicity ... and above all, a never-ending cultivation of gratitude and the burning desire to grow and evolve together.

No matter how bad our childhood was, how much we suffered, or how many traumas we carry in our pockets. If we really desire to heal and if we can hear the cries of our spirit, it will never be too late to rise back to our divinity, to find our way back "home," and to live a life of joy, love, and peace.

We are never alone. God is always waiting for us, with his angelic army of divine light warriors that are there to dry our tears, so that we can see clearly that we always had the keys to the prison that was keeping us captive.

In a healthy and loving relationship, Shiva and Shakti, the masculine and feminine aspects of creation, embrace each other into oneness.

The urge for completion doesn't come from the negative selfish desires of the lower ego but from the thirst for integration and communion through the fusion of two halves that complement each other.

These two halves are complete in their essential attributes. Complete male and complete female. Nothing is lacking, nothing is lost. It's all there to celebrate joy and bliss.

Every era has a polarity. The past Kali Yuga era carried the lower aspects of the male dominance, a patriarchic civilization in which divide and conquer, the rape of the planet, and the aggressive subjugation of the divine feminine were the rule.

We are now entering a new matriarchic era, in which the divine feminine is being embodied by Mother Earth. Men are learning how to be more sensitive and caring. Women are learning how to integrate and embrace their femininity without competition with their male counterparts.

When the divine feminine rules, the world gets creative, more loving, more nurturing, and more peaceful.

Every 25,500 years approximately, our sun completes a full cycle around our galaxy. This marks the collapse of a civilization and the beginning of a new era. The old must be destroyed for the new to emerge. And this is happening right now.

A new portal is being opened for us, which is a huge opportunity to evolve from baby steps to a quantum leap. It's a time to integrate all aspects of ourselves into the divine. It's a time for us to rebirth into a new race, actualizing our original divine blueprint, integrating and fully activating the twelve full strands of our DNA, and returning to our original perfection.

The return of Adam before the fall.

Our mission is to embrace this shift wholeheartedly, actualize our highest potential, unleash our creative power, and use our gifts and talents towards our happiness, the happiness of others, and the planetary liberation.

Let's welcome freedom with the birth of this new Golden Era and allow unconditional love to rule this new kingdom.

CHAPTER 22

THE MAGIC OF OUR ESSENCE

In certain old indigenous tribes, the natives were raised to honor, respect, and follow the wisdom of their elders. They lived in deep connection with nature, which is the best teacher of all.

Nature teaches by integration, communion, and the language of energy, which I call "DIRECT EXPERIENCE."

Our logical mind is constantly analyzing, labeling, judging, and trying to understand all things from an intellectual perspective.

It puts things into "boxes," and if it doesn't fit, it discards or classifies as unreal.

It's always in our way, minding matters where it doesn't belong, intruding in all areas of our life and all men affairs.

It has no capacity of abstraction nor understands the deepest mysteries of cosmic truths.

It's a limited and narrow straight shooter that knows only one horizontal linear direction, that has no curves, no design, and no artistic form.

It feels comfortable with the familiar and very uncomfortable with the unknown.

The natives use their inner senses and a deep intuition to perceive reality.

The elders were in constant connection with the Great Spirit of the earth ... rivers, forests, mountains, animals, and the five elements of creation.

The wind whispered secrets in their ears, the fire taught them the alchemy of transformation of the elements, the waters, the art of flexibility, adaptability, and the purification of the soul. The earth held them in her womb, nourishing and providing them security and sustenance.

They were bonded with the spirit of the animals, and from their innate abilities, they could shape-shift and merge with their attributes.

They learnt how to give grace and honor the vital life they received from the sun, followed the guidance of the stars, and learnt the magical mysteries of the moon.

Their ancestors were respected; the wisdom of the old shamans was honored and cultivated.

Magic was a daily ordinary occurrence. They lived in peace, unity, and integration with all living things. They were integral part of the whole eco-system and were the guardians of the forests.

What happened to us, civilized race?

How could we lose the divine link that made us humans? How could we forget all this magic?

Instead of merging with the powers of nature, we are raping and killing the earth, our mother.

Instead of creating modern technology to provide balance and harmony and preserve the integrity of our eco-environment, what did we do?

We created it for the destruction of our sacred home, for the idolatry of false gods, and the generation of soulless systems of self-enslavement.

We are helping to build a metallic civilization, "the machine kingdom," the birth of transhumanism, in which everything is artificial and devoid of organic life.

Our schools teach boring and obsolete dead sciences, designed to dumb down our children and to program them to subservience.

Our food is poisoned with pesticides, our water contaminated with chemicals, so that we can have short lives and die younger, spending fortunes to guarantee the profits of our corrupt health industry.

Whoever discovers the cure of cancer and threatens the huge profit of Big Pharma is ridiculed, suppressed, killed, or silenced.

Financial monopolies generate scarcity for everyone.

Most people are stuck working endless hours in a job they hate, just to barely survive and pay the bills.

Our elders are considered a dead weight, so they should be eliminated anyways; a virus will take care of most of them, and a synthetic experimental poisoning vaccine will eliminate or reduce the life spam of the rest of the human cattle.

5G network's harmful radiation powers a massive grid of artificial intelligence created to control and enslave the masses.

Human rights are being ripped out of the planet.

Nature is forgotten, people's souls are forgotten, life is forgotten. Our divine essence is being downgraded into a lower species. Our "clairs" are being dimmed and the voice of our spirit silenced. Welcome to the artificial matrix! Come and get an upgrade by merging your brains with electronic mind control devices. You will be smarter and more powerful than ever, beyond your wildest dreams. Who needs the spirit anyways?

This dystopian society must perish. There is so much goodness in this world, so much to live for, so much to explore, and so much to celebrate. All we need to do is open our eyes.

The sacred promised land mentioned in the Bible is here, amid this dystopian chaos. It's here inside each one of us.

We have the secrets of immortality inside our hearts, and nobody can take this power away from us.

This "Manual for Life" is a cry for freedom and a call for sovereignty.

Whoever has ears will hear and whoever has eyes will see.

And when the eyes of each one of us open, there will be no stone left in the evil empire of illusions, because immortality is our birthright.

I love you dearly, and when I'm gone from this dream world, I will remain in the words of this book, in the ideas I shared, in the thoughts and emotions imprinted on these pages.

I hope they will illuminate your paths somehow, inspire you to take ownership of your destiny, and serve as a helping guide throughout the adventures of your beautiful lives.

"May"

May the world be in peace
Children playing at ease
Laugh, joy, and happiness
No pain, poverty, or madness
May the sun light up my heart
And make me see bright and clear
Like the shine of a star
All the things I must hold dear
May my eyes never miss
The beauty we create
With the power of a kiss
May I live with no fear
May I hold no despair
May the truth be so clear
That can be sensed in the air
May I always forgive
May I let all things be
May I learn how to give
May I always be free.

Printed in the United States
by Baker & Taylor Publisher Services